HMS Drake
Rathlin Island Shipwreck

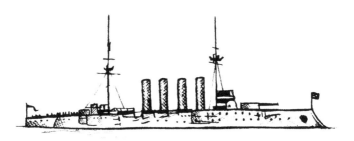

HMS Drake
Rathlin Island Shipwreck

Ian Wilson

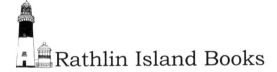

Rathlin Island Books

First published in 2011 by Rathlin Island Books.

Distributed by Rathlin Island Books.

RIB #01

ISBN: 978-0-9568942-0-5

Printed by Impact Printing, Ballycastle, Co Antrim (www.impact-printing.co.uk).

Cover art: original painting by Kenneth King (www.king-studio.com).

Inside sketch of HMS *Drake* by Barbara Henderson.

Cover painting photographed by Tom McDonnell (admin2.clikpic.com/tommcdonnell).

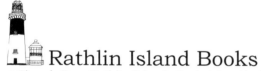

Rathlin Island Books
4 Church Bay, Rathlin Island, Co Antrim, Northern Ireland, BT54 6SA.
www.rathlinislandbooks.com

Contents

Acknowledgements

I would like to express warm thanks to the following, who contributed information, anecdotes, technical insights, and exciting diving experiences:
Robert Anderson, Steen Anderson, Richard Bennett, Commander Peter Campbell, Douglas Cecil, Mary Cecil, John Cole, Commonwealth War Graves Commission, Francis Cox, Johnny Curry, Derry City Museum Service (Craig McGuicken), Wes Forsythe, Dr David Jenkins, Loughie McCuaig, Bert McDowell, Neil McFaul, Loughie McQuilkin, Commander Gilbert Mayes, Jean Molloy, Danny Morgan, Richard Perceval-Maxwell, Alison Plumridge, Leonard Quigg, Frank Rogers, Southampton City Council Archives (Joanne Smith), and Iain Wysner.

I would also like to acknowledge the extensive research work undertaken by the late Tommy Cecil. The oral narratives of islanders featured in this book were collected by him, and add a richness to this story that otherwise would not have been possible to recount after all this time.

Stephen Ryan and Jessica Bates of Rathlin Island Books brought as much encouragement as any author could wish for to all aspects of this book's concept and writing.

And thank you to Stephen, Jessica and the people of Rathlin Island for their frequent hospitality!

Foreword

The ever changing seas and tides of Rathlin have claimed over 60 documented shipwrecks, but of all the ships to be lost HMS *Drake* would be the most significant. The events of 2 October 1917 have now all but faded into Rathlin's maritime history.

My first dive onto HMS *Drake* was at the age of fourteen diving with my father the late Tommy Cecil. Descending the shotline onto the wreck at a depth of thirteen metres, my first view of the wreck was the barrel of one of the six inch guns pointing upwards, the wreck being a complex mass of twisted armoured plating and steel framing heavily coated in concretion and thick kelp with shoals of lythe and glashon fish darting through the many openings of the wreck. The sheer size of the wreck seemed to stretch as far as you could see. Now – having returned from a career at sea to ply Rathlin's waters – every time I pass south of the wreck buoy I am reminded of that first encounter with the *Drake*.

This book is about more than the loss of a ship, it depicts life at the peak of naval supremacy within the British Empire, in a period of technological advances in ship design and changing warfare tactics, and the decisions taken by the men involved, from HMS *Drake*'s Captain Stephen Radcliffe escorting convoy HH 24, to his adversary Kapitänleutnant Rohrbeck of *U 79* lying in wait off Rathlin.

In writing this book, Ian Wilson has been able to capture the story of HMS *Drake* in such a way that the reader gets a real insight into the lives of the men who built the ship in Pembroke Dock, through to the men who served on her and those on her final day on convoy escorting duties, and the Rathlin Islanders who witnessed the last moments of HMS *Drake*.

D. C

Douglas Cecil
Rathlin Island
April 2011

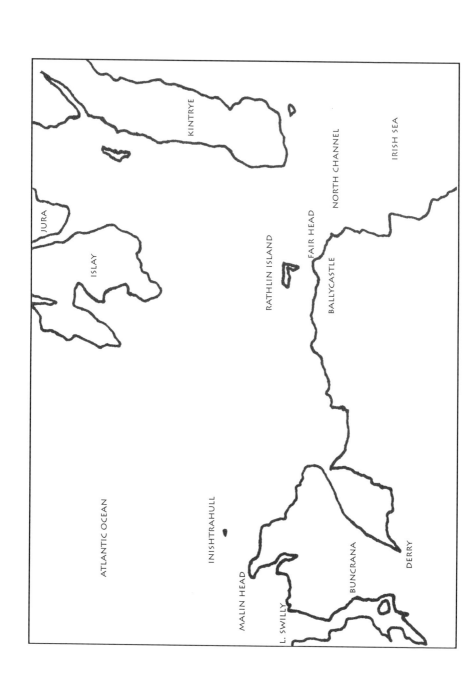

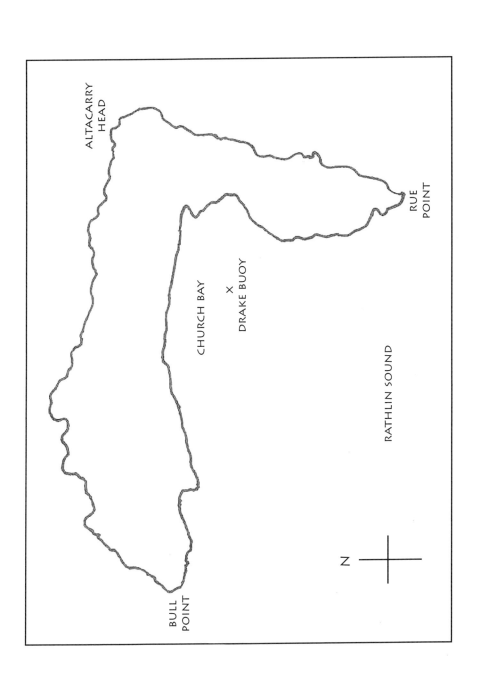

INTRODUCTION
The Great Wreck in the Bay

In the summer of 1920, it was a long way from a vicarage in the village of Wadhurst in Sussex to a new life as Rector on Rathlin Island off the north coast of Ireland. This is the post which the Rev Leslie Creevy Stevenson accepted with his wife and young son Patric, and the move which Letitia Stevenson chronicles in 'The Guttering Candle; or, Life on Rathlin 1920 – 1922':

> …the house doors are painted green and white, there are a few little paths covered with black and white pebbles, the walls around are about six foot high, and there is a nice little bit of lawn in front of the door. When Patric wants a hot bath he has it here with a good-sized tub and kettles of boiling water. Of course, the sea is the usual bath for us all… nice stones can be picked up all over the island, white ones predominate. Church Bay is quite dazzlingly white, and the sea anemones are wonderful. All colours, vermilion, orange, crimson, green and brown…

But they soon found that the tranquillity of island life was being disturbed. In the middle of Church Bay:

> …lies a long, curved object like a great whale over which the waves break incessantly. It is the corpse of H.M.S. *Drake*, torpedoed in 1917, she reeled about like a drunken man after she was hit and finally sank here. Only her bilge keel can now be seen. The islanders say there are 19 stokers' bodies still in her…

Now a salvage team was at work. Explosives were regularly being detonated. On the quay opposite where the Stevensons' possessions had been unloaded from small boats from Ballycastle, lay a tangled assortment of scrap waiting to be shipped away. Cordite from the ship's magazines lay in piles on the shore. Clad in their outlandish hard hats, divers plunged off the salvage boat *Mary*. It was the biggest event to happen to Rathlin in centuries, possibly, and with chilling irony, since Francis Drake aided the Elizabethan soldier and adventurer Sir John Norris in a massacre of islanders. Now the Royal Navy cruiser named after him lay sunk in Church Bay.

…the islanders have plenty of gossip about the *Drake*. The Captain was a German spy, he had lost three other ships… he could easily have taken her to Larne or Derry but he just fooled about and lost her…

This needless to say does Captain Radcliffe and the officers a grave disservice! From being torpedoed by *U 79* five miles north of the island to capsizing in the bay, all their decisions were good ones. Nearly 900 men were safely evacuated. The Admiralty were to attach no blame to anyone. But it is a story that has never been told in detail before, the story of a single day, Tuesday 2 October 1917, that not only saw the loss of the biggest ship – to this day – to lie close to the Irish coast, and one which attracts many sport divers annually, but also the loss of two other ships to the mines of the intrepid Kapitänleutnant Rohrbeck in *U 79* – not to mention a collision which led to a fascinating legal case. And the cordite is still occasionally exploded by the island youth!

The forlorn wreck of the *Drake* which the Stevensons happened upon had been among the largest and finest warships of her era. She sailed most of the seven seas, flying an Admiral's flag in Australia, and a Prince's around the Mediterranean and across the Atlantic. Greek and Spanish Royals were entertained, and Edward VII spent a night aboard. She was anchored in the Bay of Naples when Vesuvius erupted, and was the venue for the grandest of balls in New York harbour. Her heyday coincided with the zenith of British sea power, when the King was on the throne, the pound was worth a pound, W G Grace was batting in front of a full house on a sunny day at Lord's, and the fleet was steaming up the Channel…

CHAPTER ONE
A Swift Battleship in Disguise

The naval town of Pembroke Dock in south-west Wales was en fête on 3 March 1901. Almost every working man was employed in the shipyard, so it was a tradition that for launches routine ceased for the occasion: schools and shops closed, and a celebratory air pervaded the streets. On this day, just four weeks after the nation had seemed to stand still for the funeral of Queen Victoria, Pembroke Dock and the Royal Navy were marking the launch of the huge armoured cruiser HMS *Drake*. In the 1890s Pembroke Dock had constructed battleships with grand, resounding names like *Empress of India*, *Renown* and *Hannibal*, but not only did the new ship bear a name as illustrious as any in British naval history, she was the longest ship ever built at the yard, 533 feet (162 metres) and one of the longest warships in the world.

Pembroke Dock nowadays is one of those places which history seems to have left behind. Situated a few miles from Pembroke town itself, little remains to remind the visitor that this had been an important Admiralty dockyard town, which built over 250 ships for the Royal Navy between 1816 and 1926, adapting well to the vast technological changes in that time, from sail to steam, from wood to iron and then steel. Decline set in a few years after completion of the *Drake*, when Admiral Sir John Fisher became First Sea Lord and commenced sweeping reforms, but when the *Drake* was on the stocks about 2,500 workers were employed at Pembroke Dock. It was a tightly-knit, settled community, looking forward to the 20th century and the new Edwardian era with confidence. Electricity had arrived and the yard had its own power station. The work was not well paid, but it was secure and pensionable, although shipbuilding had more than its share of industrial accidents: John Lewis, aged 56, Established Labourer number 595, was painting a bulkhead in the port engine room of the *Drake* on 30 January 1901 when he slipped and fell thirteen feet on to the engine bearings and then into the crankpit. He fractured his skull, which resulted in total deafness 'in addition he lost his left eye when building HMS *Shannon* on 1 May 1875', recorded Fleet Surgeon

Edward Luther, 'and his capacity to contribute to his own support is destroyed.' That was the same month when the Admiralty announced that the families of those killed in Naval dockyards would henceforth have to pay for the deceased's coffin.

By this time the ship had been under construction for nearly two years, having been laid down on 24 April 1899. She was to be the first and name ship of a class of four cruisers, an evolution of the *Cressy* class in the rapid development of the world's navies. Fisher (at the time Second Sea Lord) had high hopes for these new cruisers, believing that their speed was absolutely vital, because Britain's enemies would naturally flee, their ships being weaker. They should be regarded, he said, as 'swift battleships in disguise'. Her three sisters were *Good Hope* and *Leviathan* built on Clydeside, and *King Alfred*, at Barrow. They were classed as 'armoured cruisers', fast enough to continue the cruiser tradition of patrolling global trade routes, but resilient enough with their new Krupp armoured belts to stand in the line of battle. Germany's Krupp Arms Works developed a novel type of hardened steel in the 1890s, which was soon adopted by the major navies. The headlong speed of the armaments race can be judged by the fact that at the close of the 19th century, 20,000 workers were employed by Krupp, making them the world's largest industrial company. The *Drake* and her sisters were protected by a six inch (15 cm) belt amidships, narrowing to three inches towards the bow. The turrets fore and aft for her main armament of two 9.2 inch guns were also protected by six inch steel, but the most massive armour was given to the conning tower, a full foot (30 cm). This was a small cramped cylinder below the bridge where command personnel could navigate the ship while under enemy fire.

Combining solidity and speed was the ideal for armoured cruisers, which had first entered the world's fleets in the 1870s to counteract the development of new explosive shells. Sir William White, Director of Naval Construction, was the man responsible for the design of the *Drake* class. White (1845-1913) bore ultimate responsibility for the design of 245 Royal Navy vessels, including 26 armoured cruisers, but it was a spectacular mishap to another ship at Pembroke Dock near where the *Drake* was being built which led to his early retirement. The new Royal Yacht *Victoria and Albert*, no less, was being floated out of a drydock on 3 March 1900 when she almost capsized (reputedly due to instability caused by extra cement sound-proofing the Royal quarters).

Mortified, White left the Admiralty but returned to eminence as consulting architect for the great Cunard liner *Mauretania* a few years later. His design for the *Drake* class and similar cruisers was criticised as their secondary armament of six inch guns, housed in barbettes set in to the side of the hull, could only be used in relatively calm conditions. If the ship was rolling, they would dip under. This was to be graphically demonstrated at the Battle of Coronel off the coast of Chile in November 1914, when the sister of the *Drake*, the *Good Hope* and the similar *Monmouth* were sunk by von Spee's squadron, their six inch guns flooding in the rough seas.

But when the *Drake* was finally commissioned into the Royal Navy at Portsmouth on 13 January 1903, she was in the front rank of warships of her time. The steam reciprocating engines of her class are believed to have been the most powerful ever built. And two years later, a sea battle 12,000 miles away seemed to justify the potential of the armoured cruiser breed. Between Korea and Japan, the Tsushima Strait was the scene of history's only decisive clash fought by steel warship fleets. The Japanese fleet under Admiral Togo destroyed two-thirds of the Russian force under Admiral Rozhdestvensky, which had steamed all the way from the Baltic. Naval strategists analysed the battle avidly, and one fact which emerged was that the Japanese armoured cruiser *Nisshin* managed to stay in line despite receiving thirteen hits from heavy guns. This led to an increased number of armoured cruisers being constructed by the leading powers. However, the huge cost of the *Drake* and her sisters to the British Exchequer, depleted by the outlay on the Boer War, meant that subsequent classes were smaller. Such was the rapidity of change, however, that within a few years, as we will see later, the *Drake* and her counterparts were outclassed and superseded by the giant step forward of 'all big gun' *Dreadnought* class battleships and a fast new type, battle-cruisers.

But in 1903, the *Drake* was a major new unit which her first Captain, Francis Bridgeman, could assume was destined for a long career. After six months he was succeeded by one of the most illustrious figures in the history of the Royal Navy, John Jellicoe. Jellicoe (1859-1935), of course, went on to great things: Commander of the Grand Fleet at Jutland; First Sea Lord; Admiral of the Fleet; and ultimately Viscount Jellicoe of Scapa. He took a typically 'hands on' approach to the ship, as surviving letters to the Captain Superintendent of Pembroke Dockyard, Rear-Admiral Barlow, reveal. Even eight months after the ship has entered service, he is in correspondence about the lack of tightness of 'watertight' doors and the consequent leaks. In fact, Jellicoe came to believe that new warships had worrying weaknesses caused by what we would now call technology. The meticulous Jellicoe examined the ship in detail, but he was perturbed.

Drake and her sisters were no longer properly watertight below deck, owing to the ever-increasing number of electrical cables, leads, voicepipes, water conduits and fuel pipes passing through the bulkheads. His fears may have been justified after the *Drake* was torpedoed as will be related later. It was several decades before effective sealant was invented to minimise such leaks.

But the ship that he now commanded was an imposing member of the Fleet, costing a little over £1 million, a gigantic sum then. Her triple-expansion coal-fired engines drove two propellers and burned an average of eleven tons of coal per hour, working up to twenty tons per hour for the maximum speed of 24 knots. The class were always regarded as good steamers, which often exceeded their trials performance. The hot and arduous labour of feeding the powerful engines was the domain of the stokers, no fewer than 300 of them labouring in four boiler rooms – a third of the ship's company! That included more skilful jobs done by the Petty Officer Stokers and Chief Stokers, who needed to know more than the men trimming, who brought the coal in wheelbarrows to the furnaces, and the firemen, although their job required careful judgment to keep the fires at the optimum level. Deafened, sweating and toiling at the best of times, duty for the 'black gang' in the stokeholds during a battle can barely be imagined, and of course it was they who were most at risk from the new weapon, the torpedo. It was in Boiler Room Two that all the fatalities happened when *Drake* was hit off Rathlin.

The ship under Jellicoe celebrated Christmas 1903 at Las Palmas and then with *Good Hope*, *Donegal* and *Kent* sailed for Barbados. Three months were spent cruising the West Indies before a return to Portsmouth via Bermuda. After exercises in the Channel, the cruiser squadron sailed for the Mediterranean. Jellicoe left in November 1904, replaced by Captain Sturdee, later to be the victor over von Spee at the Battle of the Falklands.

Remarkably, one example of an armoured cruiser similar to the *Drake* still exists. Greek Navy crews are ordered to attention today as their ship passes the *Georgios Averof* moored as a floating museum at Faliron, a suburb of Athens. Still regarded as in active service and flying a Rear-Admiral's flag, the three-funnelled *Georgios Averof* was built at Livorno in Italy in 1911 and during a long career until 1952 served from the First Balkan War against the Ottoman Turks through to patrol duties in the Indian Ocean with the Allies in World War Two. A shorter warship at 140 metres, she is otherwise comparable to the *Drake* in armour, armament and performance.

Three other smaller cruisers from the era still exist, with HMS *Caroline* in Belfast the last survivor of the Battle of Jutland: taken for granted of course by most of those who are familiar with the ancient grey profile berthed near the Science Park in the new 'Titanic Quarter', but a remarkable survivor too, little changed and retaining a distinct atmosphere of the Navy at the time of Jellicoe, especially below deck. Only in December 2009 did she relinquish her role as the base for the local Royal Naval Reserve (RNR) and future plans are currently undecided. In St Petersburg, the *Aurora* of 1903 is a revered symbol of the Russian revolution, being the ship which fired the first shots in the 1917 uprising. While at Independence Seaport Museum, Philadelphia, the *Olympia* is designated a National Historic Landmark, but in need of extensive hull repairs, inevitable given her age as she was completed in 1892, when her steam engines, being the more efficient triple-expansion, were still novel. It was such engines that powered the *Drake* – mighty ones in her case – but by the time *Caroline* was commissioned in December 1914, oil-fired Parsons turbines were well established, such were the relentless sweeping innovations in the world of sea power.

It was an era of change recorded vividly in the absorbing diaries of the engaging Admiral George King-Hall, who flew his flag in the *Drake* out in Australia, and had a very close Ulster connection. He was married to Olga Ker, branches of whose family owned estates at Montalto, outside Ballynahinch, and Portavo, near Donaghadee. Olga's sister Nini, moreover, owned Quintin Castle near Portaferry and the King-Halls spent much time there. When George King-Hall was Senior Naval Officer in Ireland, based at Queenstown (Cobh) the gunboat HMS *Colleen* would regularly convey the family 250 miles to Quintin and land them for a holiday at the Castle – not something expenses would be allowed to cover nowadays! But the high point of his career came in 1912 when he was appointed Senior Naval Officer in Australia, with his flagship being the *Drake*.

CHAPTER TWO
Cruising the Seas of the Empire

The band of HMS *Drake* played 'A Life on the Ocean Wave' as their Captain, Edward Bruen, and his new bride, Constance Drummond, passed through the 200 happy guests massed around the sundial on the lawn of Admiralty House, Sydney. It was 14 September 1912, a sunny day, to the relief of Admiral George King-Hall, Commander-in-Chief, Australia, who recorded the events in his diary.

As the newly-weds moved among the throng, bridesmaids Madge and Lou King-Hall and Molly Street scattered rose petals in their path, and when they reached the jetty to return to the *Drake,* floating at anchor in the magnificence of Sydney Harbour, her officers were there lining the water's edge, sending them off with three rousing cheers. 'So ended a most successful Naval wedding,' records the Admiral, 'two people eminently suited for each other, and, I ask God, that they may be much blessed through their married life.'

Admiral King-Hall and his wife Olga had a particularly keen interest in the wedding of the Captain of the flagship and the shy Miss Drummond – an Admiral's daughter herself – as they had match-made a few months earlier! 'We arranged something every day to throw her and Captain Bruen together,' he notes, but the actual engagement required a signal from Admiralty House to the *Drake* for Captain Bruen to come ashore, and a man-to-man talk, because Constance was too reserved to let her feelings show to the Captain!

The *Drake* arrived in Australia in February 1912. Admiral King-Hall's diaries frequently mention her in their fascinating depiction of the pinnacle of Imperial power and splendour, the Admiral being second only to the Governor-General in prestige and influence.

The flagship conveyed him all round the Australian coast, and also on a cruise to New Caledonia and Fiji. A lifetime on the Seven Seas, encountering cannibalism, slavery and all manner of adventure, had not blunted the Admiral's keen interest in all he saw there.

Inevitably, bad weather was encountered too:

> 28 March 1912. Left Hobart at 4 a.m. Running full speed trial, vibrating very much, a beam sea. Touched 21 knots, Newcastle coal not so good as Welsh, otherwise would have gone to 24. All the ladies and servants down. Olga's cabin where she is with Madge very bad, great vibration and motion. Glad to get back to comforts of Admiralty House.

George King-Hall's Naval career extended from 1863 to 1914, coinciding with the heyday of the British Empire, when it is said to have comprised a quarter of the world's land mass and a quarter of its population. It was Britain's powerful Navy which allowed it to expand, patrol and protect such global possessions. When the *Drake* was laid down the arms race with Germany was just commencing, a technological and industrial rivalry which increased tension leading up to the First World War and resulted in *Drake* and her sisters being close to obsolete in 1914.

The pace of change was rapid. A significant development with which King-Hall was closely involved was the formation of the Royal Australian Navy, and references to the politics of this abound in the Australian years of his diary. He was the final Royal Navy Senior Officer on the station. On 4 October 1913, the new 'Australian Fleet Unit' entered Sydney Harbour, to the acclaim of a multitude of sightseers, headed by the new battle-cruiser *Australia* , a huge three-funnelled warship built by John Brown at Clydebank and probably still the most magnificent ship ever to serve in the Royal Australian Navy. On that day, flagship of the Australia Station was transferred from HMS *Cambrian*, the successor to the *Drake*, to *Australia*. Flying his flag in her was Rear-Admiral Sir George Patey, knighted on her deck by King George V before they left Portsmouth, and the Captain was none other than Stephen Herbert Radcliffe, later central to our story on an October morning off Rathlin when he commanded *Drake*.

Radcliffe and Patey are officially listed as 'lent from the Royal Navy' in the Australian Navy List, there being an initial period when Australian officers were still rising to the command of major warships. Radcliffe, like Bruen, King-Hall and all these men was a lifetime Naval man: from the Mediterranean to India; from the Somali coast to Australia.

He was born on 19 February 1874 to Herbert and Adria Radcliffe, who resided in the quiet seaside resort of Clevedon, Somerset. Aged only 12, he joined HMS *Britannia*, the old 'wooden wall' training ship at Dartmouth as a cadet and by 1894 was a Lieutenant. By 1904, aged 30, he had attained the rank of Commander. This was just after his involvement in the Somaliland campaign, where the British were again clashing with their long-time foe Muhammad Abdullah Hassan, the 'Mad Mullah' himself, and his Dervish movement.

It was 1920 before the Dervishes were defeated – when aircraft were first used against them – but the Royal Navy in the decades leading up to the First World War usually exerted its might to ensure Britain's will was done. A classic example of this 'gunboat diplomacy' occurred in 1899 and involved Constance Drummond's father, Admiral Edmund Charles Drummond. The Sultan of Oman was made aware that Her Britannic Majesty's Government was displeased. In fact, were he not to reverse his decision to let the French coal their warships at the port of Muscat, Admiral Drummond aboard HMS *Eclipse*, flagship of the East Indies Squadron, would bombard the town's forts. History records that the Sultan 'completely acquiesced to British demands'!

Admiral King-Hall refers to the marriage being 'a Naval wedding' and Naval families (generations of King-Halls served) often inter-married. The class system was also an element. It would simply have been considered natural that Constance Drummond married an officer of senior rank. Captain Bruen, son of the MP for Co Carlow, was an ideal match for Constance, great-grand-daughter of Viscount Strathallan. Her brother Ian (1873-1926) attained the rank of Vice-Admiral. Captain Bruen, who had been fourteen when he was sent to Dartmouth from the Bruen estate at Oak Park, Carlow, went on to command the battleship *Bellerophon* at the Battle of Jutland, firing over 60 rounds from her main armament and receiving no hits, ('during the afternoon the ship steamed as she had never steamed before' he reported) and concluded the war as Aide-de-Camp to the King. In the early 1920s the family settled at Halesworth, Suffolk, and the son that was born to Constance in 1918, Francis, won the DSC at Dunkirk in HMS *Jaguar* and served on the Royal Yacht *Britannia* in the 1950s. (Constance enjoyed a very long life and can last be traced living in a hotel in Bayswater, London, in 1976. Perhaps the famously hot summer of that year reminded her of Australian days).

But the most exalted figure to fly his flag in the *Drake* was Rear-Admiral Prince Louis of Battenberg, husband to a grand-daughter of Queen Victoria, and father of Earl Mountbatten of Burma. The *Drake*, leading the Second Cruiser Squadron, with her consorts *Cumberland*, *Essex*, *Cornwall*, *Berwick* and *Bedford* undertook a two-year commission in 1905-07 showing the flag round the Mediterranean and then across the Atlantic to Canada and the USA. This cruise is a glittering example of the prestige of the Royal Navy in Edwardian times. The Prince made an immense impression on the Americans, meeting President Roosevelt, and being feted wherever he went. A grand ball for the elite of New York society was held aboard *Drake*, but what the 'lower deck' would never forget was the party on 13 November 1905 thrown by the US North Atlantic Fleet's enlisted men at Stauch's dance-hall, Coney Island. Reputedly, 20,000 bottles of beer were drunk! The Prince and his counterpart Admiral Robley Evans attended, but: '…shortly after their departure all semblance of order vanished…the beer flowed like water…a vaudeville entertainment was provided but nobody listened…' The *Drake* and the other coal-fired warships carried a huge complement of stokers, a particularly thirsty type of man!

Prince Louis later sent a superb silver cup, the Battenberg Cup, to Admiral Evans for cutter racing challenges. It was aboard USS *West Virginia* when she was sunk at Pearl Harbor in 1941, but was found when she was raised and is to this day still awarded, not for cutter racing but to the crew in the United States Navy who most distinguish themselves.

The visit to the Hudson River, New York, brought thousands of sightseers swarming aboard *Drake*, billed as 'the crack cruiser in the British Navy', every small movable object being taken by souvenir hunters, one man even scaling the mast to snip off a portion of Prince Louis' flag. A soccer match between Columbia University and a team from HMS *Bedford* attracted an astonishing 30,000 spectators, and altogether the stay of the Second Cruiser Squadron in New York was a dizzying round of engagements, culminating in a sparkling ball on *Drake*, at which, among the 1,200 guests were 'the flower of beauty, talent and wealth of New York'. Ashore, Prince Louis mingled with the Astors, the Vanderbilts and their affluent friends, dining 'on the famed Astor gold dinner service', while Anglo-American relations were further strengthened when Private Cockayne, a Royal Marine from *Drake*, challenged an American to a boxing bout 'contrary to the wishes of our officers', at Tom Sharkey's club. (Cockayne knocked his adversary out!)

As the squadron was about to leave, generous words from Admiral Evans were published in the 'New York City Journal': 'It is my belief that never before in the history of any country has so large a body of sailors been entertained in so thoroughly satisfactory a manner…'

When the commission ended in May 1907 it was described by Minter, the Signal Boatswain on *Drake* who recorded it in marvellous detail, as 'the happiest and not least eventful in the history of our modern Navy'. Lofty words, but these Edwardian years were indeed the zenith of the Royal Navy. The cruise had started at Portsmouth in February 1905 with a visit and overnight stay aboard *Drake* by Edward VII himself, and a departure for Gibraltar two days later, and concluded back at Portsmouth after Prince Louis left at Gibraltar to hoist his flag in the battleship *Venerable*. Among many vivid highlights were a visit to the *Drake* by the King and Queen of Spain at Malaga, carrying Prince Andrew and Princess Alice of Greece (parents of the present Duke of Edinburgh) before the opening of the 1906 Olympic Games in Athens, and entering the Bay of Naples while Vesuvius was erupting. Let's trust that just as happy memories were of a visit to Irish waters in August 1906, firstly to Bangor Bay:

> …the *Drake* was usually open to visitors from 1 pm to sunset, and several steamers landed their passengers aboard. It was estimated that on one occasion over 2,000 visitors were aboard at the same time. The members of the Royal Ulster Yacht Club (RUYC), bent on making sport, considerately gave a prize of £5 to the winning tug-of-war team, which contest took place on their lawn at the club house, before a large and fashionable assemblage…

The Lord Mayor of Belfast hosted officers and men, conveyed by special train, to a garden party in Botanic Gardens, massed bands played on shore, a special Naval night was staged at the Theatre Royal, Belfast, and on the departure of the squadron the RUYC bade farewell to Prince Louis and his ships with a fifteen-gun salute. Lough Swilly was the next destination ('the Earl of Shaftesbury generously placed his moors at the disposal of the officers') and then the Shannon estuary, after which speed trials were run in the Atlantic. Nasty heavy seas were breaking over the bow of *Drake*, but she worked up to 23.2

knots, the scores of stokers shovelling good Welsh coal, more efficient than the Australian bunkers supplied a few years later!

The wonderful account of these days of Empire 'The Cruise of H.M.S. *Drake*' was written by the Signal Boatswain, Joseph A. Minter, to whom posterity owes a debt of thanks! Minter, who was born in Ballycotton, Co Cork, about 1865, was a Warrant Officer in charge of all the visual signalling aboard the cruiser. He concludes that this was: '...a period of service for King and Country of lifelong and affectionate remembrance for those who served in this Cruise of H.M.S. *Drake* ...'

The *Drake* came back to Bangor Bay for a week in July 1907, arriving from the Naval base of Berehaven and sailing to an anchorage off Portrush, thence Moville, Galway Bay and back to Berehaven. Interestingly, serving as Chaplain aboard the ship was none other than a man with strong Rathlin connections, Rev Alexander Gage MA, of the landowning family for so long associated with the Manor House, but he had moved on by the time of her demise in Church Bay, Rathlin Island.

In October 1908 the *Drake* returned to Ulster waters, not far from where she would end her days, when she anchored again off Portrush. The schoolboys of the nearby Coleraine Academical Institution played a rugby match against the ship, and a few days later, being granted a half-day by their formidable Headmaster Mr Houston (seemingly a figure in the Jellicoe mould) a party toured the ship:

> ...few of us but were impressed by the immense capacity of this vessel – the number of compartments and passages and ladders seemed to be endless. Special interest was taken in the guns, and our guides were untiring in their efforts to satisfy our curiosity about their mechanism. While we were aboard a display of torpedo firing took place, which was eagerly watched by a number of us who were lucky enough to be in the vicinity. At four o'clock we were entertained to tea by the officers, a repast to which we did ample justice after our dose of sea air. At half-past five we were all aboard the pinnace again, reluctantly enough, for we had a ripping time... lighted on our way by one of the searchlights, we reached land without further adventure...

The *Drake* and her sisters, while proudly showing the flag, were of course primarily fighting ships, and as the pace of change in warship design accelerated through the Edwardian years, their threat as front-line units diminished. All existing major warships were immediately superseded when Britain launched the *Dreadnought* in 1906, with hitherto unheard-of armament and steam turbines instead of coal-fired engines. Rapid technological innovation in range-finding and salvo direction meant that the *Dreadnought* and her sisters, and their German counterparts when that country caught up, could engage at ranges previously impossible. First Sea Lord Sir John Fisher (to whom George King-Hall had been Chief of Staff when Fisher was C in C Mediterranean) was mainly responsible for propelling Britain into the lead in the Naval race through his reforming energies. Soon a new type of cruiser, enthusiastically favoured by Fisher, who, as we saw earlier, liked speed, served further to supersede the *Drake* class: faster, more powerful 'battle-cruisers', of which *Australia* was an example.

In response, the Kaiser and Admiral von Tirpitz embarked on an enormously ambitious and costly programme of warship construction, expenditure rising to a staggering 24% of the entire national budget in 1908. There was no doubt now who Britain's main naval rival was. Let us therefore leave the perception of the spirit of the age, in German the zeitgeist, to King-Hall, at this time Senior Royal Navy Officer, Ireland, based in Queenstown, writing in his diary on 22 April 1908: '…Field Marshall Lord Grenfell agreed with me that the Germans considered an invasion of England perfectly feasible, and were not losing a chance of perfecting every last detail of it…'

HMS *Drake*. (Imperial War Museum, Q21180)

Top left: Admiral Sir John Jellicoe, second Captain of the *Drake*. (*Imperial War Museum, Q67791*)

Centre: Wedding party of Captain Edward Bruen and Constance Drummond, Sydney 1912. (*Courtesy of Richard Perceval-Maxwell*)

Bottom right: Admiral Sir George King-Hall and Stephen King-Hall, 1908. (*Courtesy of Richard Perceval-Maxwell*)

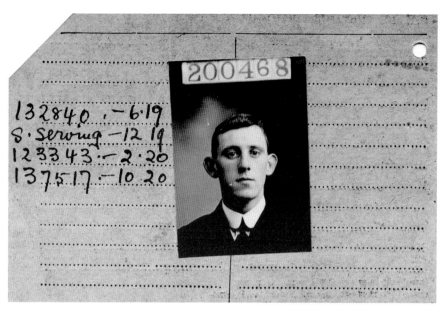

132840. - 6.19
S. Serving - 12 19
123343. - 2.20
137517 - 10 20

200468

Above: Apprentice Cyril
Beadnell Potts, from
his Identity Certificate.
(*Southampton Archives*)

Left: Philip Danby Collin.
(*Courtesy of Alison Plumridge*)

Captain Stephen Herbert Radcliffe.
(*National Maritime Museum, Greenwich, P2260*)

Kapitänleutnant Otto Rohrbeck.
(*Bundesarchiv, Bild 146-1994-116-08A*)

Drake-class armoured cruiser and other Royal Navy
warships in Lough Swilly, Co Donegal. (*Courtesy of The
National Library of Ireland, L_ROY_09300 & L_ROY_09299*)

Above: *U 79*. (*Bilddienst Archives, 10349*)
Below: *U 79*'s map of mining activities, September 1917. (*Tommy Cecil Collection, Courtesy of Mary Cecil*)

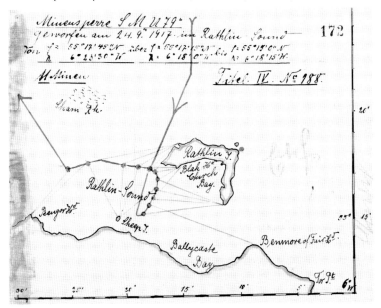

Crew being taken off the sinking HMS *Drake* in Church Bay, Rathlin. (*Tommy Cecil Collection*)

CHAPTER THREE
August 1914: Castles of Steel

Captain Stephen Radcliffe had no doubt of the fighting power of his ship, the battle-cruiser *Australia*. Nor did Admiral Maximilian von Spee. In fact, he worried that she alone was superior to his entire cruiser force. Von Spee's German East African Squadron was based in Tsingtao, a German possession on the Chinese coast. To avoid being trapped there, he planned an epic return to Germany through the Pacific and around Cape Horn. As the *Australia* escorted the Australian Naval and Military Expeditionary Force on their mission to capture German wireless stations in New Guinea and Samoa – critics said a bolder plan would have been to seek the German ships, although before radar or air spotting the Pacific was an even more vast place – von Spee was bound from Tahiti towards South America. Off the coast of Chile, he was brought to battle by the dashing Admiral Sir Christopher Cradock, leading HMS *Good Hope*, one of the two sisters of the *Drake*, and HMS *Monmouth*, a similar but smaller cruiser.

Cradock did not intend to experience the shame of Admiral Ernest Troubridge, who had been court-martialled for failing to engage the enemy, even though the odds heavily disadvantaged him. But the *Good Hope* and the *Monmouth* were out-gunned and out-manoeuvred. Both went down with all hands – 1,570 British officers and men. Von Spee was presented with a bouquet of flowers by the German community in Valparaiso, Chile, but he tersely responded by stating they would do nicely on his grave. He knew that retribution by the Royal Navy was inevitable, and he was 12,000 miles from home. Five weeks later, his force was destroyed at the Battle of the Falklands, mainly by two fast new battle-cruisers similar to the *Australia*, the *Inflexible* and *Invincible*. A former Captain of the *Drake*, Doveton Sturdee, commanded the victorious squadron.

The loss of the *Good Hope* and *Monmouth,* and the equally catastrophic sinking of the cruisers *Aboukir*, *Cressy* and *Hogue* in the North Sea by the submarine *U 9* in three hours cruelly demonstrated the vulnerability of these older units. This had been feared. Battle-cruisers and *Dreadnought* battleships were the future. After the *Drake* had returned to Britain from her role as King-Hall's Australian flagship, she was placed in reserve. However, the pressure of coming hostilities earned her a new commission, and she was re-activated just in time for a grand fleet review by King George V at Spithead on 18 July 1914. It was a test mobilisation, and a few weeks later Britain and Germany were indeed at war.

Submarines and the laying of mines, the elements of naval warfare that combined to destructive effect the day the *Drake, Brisk* and *Lugano* were sunk off Rathlin, shocked the British. Winston Churchill, First Lord of the Admiralty, famously used the chilling phrase 'the live bait squadron' for the vulnerable *Aboukir*, *Cressy* and *Hogue* and in consultation with the First Sea Lord (the Chief of Naval Staff), the rank to which Prince Louis of Battenberg had now been elevated, had agreed they should be withdrawn from the North Sea. No more modern ships were available, however, and the apprehensions of the Admiralty were borne out only four days later.

Reaction to the use of the new weapons of war was expressed in the statement of startling frankness made by the Admiralty after the loss of the three cruisers:

> …modern naval war is presenting us with many new and strange situations… although they were large powerful ships, they belonged to a class of cruiser whose speeds had been surpassed by many of the enemy's battleships. Before the war it had been decided that no more money should be spent repairing any of this class…

'We despised the mine and considered it a weapon no civilised nation would use' stated a Naval staff monograph, while Admiral Tyrwhitt, Commander of the Harwich squadron of destroyers, grumbled 'it will be months before the North Sea is fit for yachting'. Another traumatic shock to the Admiralty was the loss by a single mine of the new Dreadnought battleship *Audacious* off the Donegal coast in October 1914 – and this time there was no statement, but an attempted cover-up of the event.

The loss of the 'live bait squadron' and the *Good Hope* and *Monmouth* dramatically and tragically pointed out the risks of exposing the older cruisers. But two years later, at Jutland, the great naval battle of the whole war, the armoured cruisers still suffered calamities. Admiral King-Hall's son Stephen in HMS *Southampton* witnessed the *Defence* blow up: 'she seemed to glow all over and burst in every direction...'

The failure of the Dardanelles expedition and the resulting Gallipoli campaign in 1915 led to the dismissal of Churchill as First Lord of the Admiralty. It was he who had described the new Royal Navy warships as 'Castles of Steel', and with macabre Churchillian eloquence, observed that von Spee may have humiliated the Royal Navy, but he was 'a cut flower in a vase, fair to see but bound to die.' Admiral King-Hall as Senior Officer in Australia irritated Churchill owing to his independent outlook and negotiations with Australian politicians over the proposed Royal Australian Navy. He records in his diary for 28 December 1912 Churchill's autocratic ways: '...fancy a man like Wilson, Admiral of the Fleet, who went to the post at the special request of the late King, being treated in this manner by a comparatively young man. He must be quite insufferable!'

This was Admiral Sir Arthur Wilson, VC (1842-1921) whose denigrators, it should be said, were as emphatic as his supporter King-Hall! He was known to the men as 'old 'ard 'at' and actively dissuaded officers from marrying! But with direct relevance to the shock of German submarine warfare in 1914 are his words, often quoted, which are thought to have delayed the development of British submarines: 'underhand, unfair and damned un-English!'

Thus, by the autumn of the first year of the war, Britain's Naval high command was given cause for deep reconsideration of the strengths and weaknesses of the forces at their disposal. Yet there was no Naval staff college as yet to study strategy and tactics; the spirit of Nelson was largely assumed to live on and be all that the Navy really needed. We are very fortunate that Admiral King-Hall's son Stephen, serving in the light cruiser *Southampton*, followed the family habit of keeping a journal during these momentous times. His account of the outbreak of the war is very poignant, seen in retrospect: 'it's not likely to last more than a month...' Just a few weeks previously, his ship had visited Kiel with a British squadron for the famous annual week of yacht racing. He records the mutual friendliness: 'we exchanged calls with our chummy ships the *Hannover* and *Schleswig-Holstein*... now as to the officers, a more charming or perfect set of gentlemen would be hard to find.' He witnesses a Zeppelin airship fly overhead, talks to Admiral Scheer – later to command the High Seas Fleet at Jutland – and meets a pretty girl at one of the glittering dances 'one Fraulein von Ehrlenbein of Düsseldorf'. More dances were to come 'but as the news of the assassination of the Crown Prince of Austria had just arrived, they were postponed.' The event at Sarajevo changed Europe forever.

Stephen King-Hall, a 21 year-old Sub-Lieutenant, went on to take part in all the famous North Sea actions, including being shelled by Scheer's fleet at Jutland. His diary records the war at sea, its boredom, occasional deadly peril, and the inevitable sailors' battle against bad weather. On 27 September 1914, *Southampton* is off the south coast of Norway in a hard gale when she passes his father's Australian flagship, the *Drake* in company with a destroyer and the submarine *E 5*:

> ...as may be imagined with every hatch save one battened down, life was not very comfortable. At the height of the gale I saw an interesting sight, which was the *Drake*, accompanied by a destroyer, escorting *E5*, which with *E1* had made a search down the Kattegat without seeing anything. It was interesting to note the behaviour of the three types, the *Drake* plunging heavily, the destroyer like an animated cork and the *E5* like a great rock. I heard afterwards that the *E5* got fed up with the bad weather and quietly dived and lay under for 24 hours... *E1* had completely vanished two days before, but five days later she arrived in Aberdeen, reporting engine trouble...

E 1 and *E 5* were reconnoitring as a prelude to a plan to send submarines into the Baltic. In fact, *E 1* a few weeks later made an altogether less cordial British visit to Kiel, when, after successfully penetrating the Baltic via the Skagerrak between Denmark and Sweden, she unsuccessfully attacked the cruiser *Fürst Bismarck*. It may have been un-English, but modern naval warfare had been unleashed.

CHAPTER FOUR
'Underhand, Unfair and Damn'd UnEnglish!'

Chugging and bumping along the narrow lanes of the Ards Peninsula, the new motor lorry introduced by Messrs Elliot, Portaferry merchants, had become a familiar sight in the couple of years since it had first challenged the traditional horses and carts. But in late March 1915, it was engaged on a grim purpose. Bodies in Naval uniform were washing up between Ballyquintin Point at the southern tip of the peninsula and Cloughey village. The lorry was used to convey four of them to Portaferry, where on 27 March, they were interred in the churchyard of Ballyphilip parish church in the middle of the small town, by the Rector George S Greer and Curate J Boyle. Easily spotted today are the standard War Grave headstones of Royal Marine A G Bain of Portsmouth, Seaman W A Wellstead of Lydd in Kent, and two unidentified sailors. Other men from a largely forgotten disaster lie buried further north up the Ards coast, in the quiet cemeteries of Whitechurch, outside Ballywalter, and St Andrew's, Ballyesborough, in the parish of Ballyhalbert. The reality of modern submarine aggression had reached Ulster. What had happened?

On 11 March 1915, just after 5.00 am, Kapitänleutnant Bernd Wegener in *U 27* was positioned a few miles off Corsewall Point at the entrance to Loch Ryan. He was not the first U-boat commander to penetrate the Irish Sea – Otto Hersing in *U 21* had sunk three steamers off the Lancashire coast in January, permitting the crews to abandon ship first, but the scale of Wegener's attack brought the unseen power of this new weapon into shocking focus. He manoeuvred into position to aim a torpedo at a large steamer fast approaching, bound south out of the Firth of Clyde. She was the former Elders and Fyffes passenger and fruit carrier *Bayano*, now HMS *Bayano* since her conversion into an Armed Merchant Cruiser, along with other liners. Under Commander Carr, and with a crew of over 220, the *Bayano* was fatally holed and went down in a few minutes, only 26 men surviving – some only just

– to be picked up by one of Kelly's Belfast colliers the *Balmarino*, under Captain James Foster, four hours later. Another Kelly steamer, the *Castlereagh*, had come across wreckage, oil, and bodies, and reported later that the submarine had pursued her for a time at first light. To the perennial hazards of the Irish Sea was henceforth added a new menace.

Two days later, Wegener struck again to the south, closer to the County Down coast. The tramp steamer *Hartdale* was near the South Rock lightship off Cloughey on her way with coal from Glasgow to Alexandria, when Wegener appeared on the surface off the port bow, again about first light. Captain Martin ignored the command to stop and zigzagged ahead at full speed. Twice more the German ordered him to stop, firing rockets and shells from the deck gun, until finally a torpedo was launched. The U-boat picked up most of the crew and transferred them to the nearby Swedish steamer *Heimdal*, but, although sources are vague, at least one crew man lost his life.

The ghastly sight of victims of the new conflict washing in on the tide had first been experienced on the north coast of Ulster. Again apparent to the visitor today, there are War Grave headstones, those modest oblong slabs, on Rathlin and in the churchyards of Bonamargy and Ballintoy on the mainland, for crew members of the Armed Merchant Cruiser HMS *Viknor*. She however was not a submarine victim, but is believed to have struck a mine in bad weather off Tory Island in January 1915.

It is difficult for us now to imagine the consternation these new weapons of war caused. For the first time, civilians were at risk, and soon flying machines were to impose their threat on cities. Jules Verne and H G Wells were being proved right! As early as November 1914 there was a report of a U-boat being spotted off the Co Down coast and the overnight passenger sailings from Belfast were suspended. Coast dwellers felt nervous. A farmer's wife at Bankmore near Portaferry, on answering a knock at her door late one night was, she said, asked by a foreign-looking seaman for eggs and milk, for which he paid generously before heading across the fields towards the Strangford Lough narrows. Earlier, four strange figures in naval uniforms had been encountered by a neighbour, who was struck by the unusual fragrance of cigar smoke. Stories like these, including one or two from Rathlin, have been perpetuated ever since, and some occur from World War Two, mainly around Donegal and the west of Ireland, but there is no firm evidence of U-boat men coming ashore. Spiess of *U 19*, active around Rathlin in 1918, landed on the distant islands of St Kilda and North Rona, but the only convincing story closer to civilisation is that of the elderly German guest who turned up at Miss McAdam's guesthouse in Machrihanish, Kintyre, in the 1960s, and recounted how he had more than once taken his U-boat into the secluded Clas Uig bay on the coast of Islay in the First World War, and raided the local sheep population! (And the German press did publish a photograph allegedly showing Scottish sheep carcasses hanging from the conning tower of a U-boat!)

The sinking by *U 20* of the Cunard liner *Lusitania* off the Old Head of Kinsale in May 1915 emphasised to the whole world the ruthless reality of undersea combat. But ruthless countermeasures were taken by the British Admiralty. Decoy ships, termed 'Q Ships', purporting to be innocent merchantmen, were fitted with concealed guns and patrolled around the British Isles. One of these, the *Baralong*, caused the death in controversial circumstances of Wegener five months after the *Bayano* attack. In the act of sinking the *Nicosian* west of the Scilly Islands, after ordering the crew into lifeboats, *U 27* was approached by a steamer flying the Stars and Stripes and a flag signal 'Permission to Save Life Only'. Suddenly the hidden armament was fired. As *U 27* sank, her swimming survivors, including Wegener, were shot in the water, and those Germans left aboard the *Nicosian* to place explosive charges, cornered and murdered. The '*Baralong* Affair' outraged the Germans and caused President Woodrow Wilson to ponder his pro-British stance. Indeed, the bitter memory of the German Navy extended to World War Two and the naming of the 'Wegener Flotilla' of U-boats.

The furore over the attack on the *Lusitania* caused a lull in the U-boat offensive, and in August 1915 activities around Ireland and in the English Channel ceased after two more American lives were lost in the *Arabic*. But the Germans never lost faith in the eventual triumph of submarine warfare against trade routes, imposing food shortages in Britain. The year 1916 saw on the one hand the increasingly slow attrition of the campaigns on land, and on the other, hectic activity in the German shipyards as scores of new U-boats were completed. Technology strode onwards and improvements on the small petrol-engined submarines with which the Germans began the war in

August 1914 were happening almost month by month. A new class of ocean-going diesel-powered U-boat fitted out for mine-laying as well as torpedoes was conceived, Type UE 1. *U 79* which was to sink the *Drake*, was one of eight of these built by the Vulcan yard in Hamburg. Launched on 9 April 1916 and commissioned on 26 May, her first commander, before Rohrbeck of *Drake* fame took over, was Kapitänleutnant Heinrich Jess (1884-1958), a native of Bordesholm near Kiel. In his time in charge, *U 79* laid the mine which sank the *Counsellor* five miles off Galley Head, Co Cork, in September 1916, then in a destructive mission between Boxing Day 1916 and 10 January 1917 accounted, mainly by gunfire, for no fewer than ten ships – under six different flags – between the approaches to the English Channel and the coast of Portugal. Losses everywhere were mounting for the Allies...

The new minelaying class were active around the north of Ireland, too, *U 80* laying the mine which sank another Armed Merchant Cruiser, the *Laurentic* off the mouth of Lough Swilly on 25 January 1917 with the loss of 374 lives. She was carrying £5 million in gold to Halifax, Nova Scotia, to pay for munitions received from the USA (still neutral) and Canada. Another mine from *U 80* damaged the White Star liner *Celtic* south of the Isle of Man in February. (The reason why such clear attribution of victims to specific U-boats mining missions can be made is that in 1919 the Germans handed over all their wartime mining records to try to avoid further sinkings). Laying mines had its hazards, too, and in recent years a U-boat wreck off Dunbar in eastern Scotland has been identified as that of one of this class, *U 74*, which must have had a catastrophic mishap. (Underwater footage of the wreck is now accessible on YouTube).

By February 1917, Grand Admiral von Tirpitz and the German Naval Staff had persuaded the Kaiser that unrestricted submarine warfare was the best option for achieving ultimate victory. But the outcome had a decisive counter-effect which many diplomats had predicted: on 6 April 1917, the USA entered the war. A second consequence was that the British introduced the convoy system for inward-bound merchant ships, political will, especially that of Prime Minister Lloyd George, having prevailed against the doubts of the Admiralty, who, perhaps still imbued with the spirit of Nelson, saw it as too defensive a measure.

It was to convoy escort duty that the *Drake* was assigned. Since we last encountered her, through the eyes of Lieutenant King-Hall in a raging gale off the Norwegian coast, she had been active on the West Indian and North American stations, although in the early weeks of the war she had been tasked with a rendezvous with the famous liner *Olympic*, sister of the *Titanic*, as she crossed empty from New York, escorting her to Liverpool. Another voyage was round the North Cape to Archangel, escorting the Armed Merchant Cruiser *Mantua*, mission to the Russians unknown. After an overhaul at Chatham in July 1917, *Drake*, based in Bermuda, began escorting the new convoys across the Atlantic.

On 14 September 1917, it was the sixteen ships of convoy HH 24 which formed up in the great anchorage of Hampton Roads, Virginia (HH being the code for the Hampton Roads/UK convoys). Captain Stephen Radcliffe was in command, as he had been since returning in 1915 from the Pacific, bringing the *Australia* back to join the Grand Fleet, via the Straits of Magellan, the Falkland Islands and Gibraltar. His orders were more direct now: the convoy would disperse off Malin Head in Ireland, and the *Drake* proceed to Liverpool. In early October, the old cruiser should be entering the Mersey.

At just about the same date *U 79*, skippered by Kapitänleutnant Otto Rohrbeck, was quietly pulling out of her base at Wilhelmshaven, destination, the north of Ireland…

CHAPTER FIVE
Kapitänleutnant Rohrbeck Approaches Rathlin

Convoy HH 24 was half-way across the Atlantic Ocean on 24 September 1917, the *Drake* routinely shepherding the collection of everyday tramp steamers. Her speed was reduced by two-thirds to the convoy's modest eight knots. All but one steamer, named *Mendip Range*, though, were keeping their allocated stations well – one of the factors that had made the Admiralty initially reluctant to accept convoying. Convoys were new to the crews, both Merchant and Naval, and took some getting used to, but the tactic had a long and successful history. Thirty ships in a convoy were almost as hard to find in the vastness of the ocean than a single ship. When the convoys came close to the Irish coast, some of the host of small escort vessels based in Lough Swilly would rendezvous with them. That was the plan for HH 24.

On that night, 24 September, while the islanders of Rathlin were extinguishing their oil lamps, Kapitänleutnant Otto Rohrbeck was navigating his submarine *U 79* southwards, passing close by Bull Point at the west end of the island, and creeping on across Rathlin Sound to a point close inshore to Ballintoy on the mainland. Here he turned back on his course, and, heading for Bull Point again, the crew went to work laying (or as the Germans termed it, 'throwing') eight mines one by one across the western entrance to the Sound. *U 79* then was directed farther west and laid another four of her load of 32 between Bull Point and the Giant's Causeway. This is how German mining – which sank or damaged 595 ships – was undertaken: the mines with their anchor and a mooring cable were dropped to the seabed through a vertical hatch. To avoid the obvious risk to the submarine, a soluble chemical timer delayed the release upwards of the mine. When that took effect, the mine rose gradually, uncoiling its mooring wire from inside the 'sinker' or anchor, until it reached a point calculated to be fifteen feet below the surface at low tide. To balance the submarine's 'trim', compensating tanks were flooded as the mines were released and their weight lost. All these were skilled and dangerous tasks, and at the same time *U 79* was in Rathlin waters, *UC 55* was lost off Lerwick in the Shetlands when these tanks were flooded too soon. And just a few weeks before (although these events were often not pieced together for years afterwards) *UC 42* had sunk herself off the County Cork coast, probably through a disastrous failure of the timer. Her wreck was located by an oil slick at the end of October, and visited by a Naval diver, who found the stern completely blown off, indicating one of her mines had detonated under it. Only in November 2010 was *UC 42* found again by sport divers, close to Roche's Point at the entrance to Cork Harbour. They returned to leave a plaque in memory of Oberleutnant zur See Müller and his crew of 27 who went down with her, and the story and underwater footage featured on the RTÉ News. But the story does not end there. *UC 42* had laid mines off the coast of Co Waterford in June. The British were aware their code for reporting cleared mines had been broken, so when they found the minefield they reported it cleared – when in fact it was not. Misled, the Germans sent *UC 44* into the same area and she was sunk either by one of the earlier mines or one of her own on 4 August 1917, although Kapitänleutnant Tebbenjohanns made an amazing escape without any breathing apparatus. Such were the perils and adventures of early submariners.

Rohrbeck had returned to seas he knew. In the previous June, having succeeded Jess in command, he brought *U 79* to the north coast of Donegal and laid mines which claimed the Allan Liner *Carthaginian,* Glasgow for Montreal, just to the north of Inishtrahull, and two of the Lough Swilly-based Admiralty trawlers. The *Corientes* and *Charles Astie* went down off Malin Head and Fanad Head respectively. Returning round the Hebrides and north of the Shetlands to base, he sank by torpedo the British tramp steamer *Serapis,* taking the Captain and Chief Officer prisoner, and three small Swedish fishing boats.

Little is known of Otto Rohrbeck the man, apart from the fact he was born on 8 December 1882, but his career with the Imperial German Navy is well documented. Joining in 1901 at age eighteen, he was mostly engaged in coastal artillery duties until 1912, when he was promoted from Leutnant to Kapitänleutnant during service at sea in the new battleship *Oldenburg*. Early in 1916, he entered the submarine training establishment and on 15 June took command of *U 28* for less than two months before being posted as 'leader of the Navy Special

Commandos' based in the main Austro-Hungarian naval port of Pola (now Pula in Croatia). He then returned to the submarine campaign in the Atlantic.

World War One U-boats spent much more time on the surface than their successors in World War Two. In fact, they might more accurately be described as 'submersibles'. They could not go more than about 80 miles underwater before their electric motors needed re-charged (diesel engines powered the boat on the surface). In the later conflict, the development of a radar set small enough to be fitted to an aircraft made surfaced U-boats much more vulnerable. Pioneering skippers in 1914-18 were not in danger of being surprised from the air, but an American balloon station was set up at Rathmullen in Donegal, sending out patrols by these 'blimps' along the north coast, with another base near Whitehead in County Antrim. They did have the capability of dropping markers for surface craft to pursue with their rudimentary hydrophones and depth charges, but Johannes Spiess, lying submerged off Rathlin in March 1918, did not feel in the least threatened: '...the high cliffs with the barns and lighthouses were a nice picture for a painting. Around noon there were six airships in sight, which were flying up and down the cliffs with the wind, just like it was a sport...'

But Rohrbeck, Spiess and the other Germans who surreptitiously crept into these waters were certainly at risk. The British posted Vice-Admiral F S Miller to command the north-west approaches from the Naval base *Hecla* at Buncrana, and scores, indeed hundreds, of destroyers, minesweepers and armed trawlers were deployed in Lough Swilly and another naval base in Larne Lough to meet the increased U-boat menace after February 1917. They had their successes. *U 110* was sunk by the destroyers *Michael* and *Moresby* north of Fanad Head, and HM trawler *Pilot Me* and other patrol craft accounted for *UB 82* east of Rathlin, while the similar *UB 85* was sunk by another armed trawler, the *Coreopsis*, in the North Channel. When Kapitänleutnant Krech of *UB 85* was picked up, he told his captors that most of his crew were suffering from stomach complaints 'which explained their low morale and lack of resistance'. And some boats simply disappeared, such as *UB 17* which sailed from Zeebrugge on 11 March 1918 and was not heard of again.

Rohrbeck worked stealthily at night. He moved westwards and laid mines in the Sound between Inishtrahull and Malin Head. On 29 September, he is back north of Rathlin, determining to lay more of his mines off Islay. Around 11.00 pm, he spots a ship and submerges again. When it is out of sight, 'I decide to block the ship route along the area of the Maol na Ho...' (Rohrbeck's chart gave him the Gaelic name of the Mull of Oa, the southerly point of the island.) He 'throws' mines here, one of which was to have fatal consequences a few weeks later. Rohrbeck spends the next day, 30 September, surfaced between the north coast of Ireland and Islay, occasionally submerging as destroyers come in sight. He can count seven armed Naval trawlers in Inishtrahull Sound, engaged, he is sure, in sweeping mines – probably the barrage that he himself laid.

Rohrbeck had over 30 crew with him in *U 79*, enduring a cramped and smelly life confined in a steel cigar packed with a spider's web of valves, pipes, gauges, dials, pumps, meters and electrical leads. By this time they had been away from home for over a fortnight, and fuel and supply levels dictated that it would soon be time to head north again and navigate the circuitous loop away to the Shetland Islands and across the North Sea to the U-boat base at Brunsbüttel, where the Kiel Canal to the Baltic meets the North Sea.

The first day of October dawned cloudy and showery. Again Rohrbeck stations *U 79* north of Rathlin, but an uneventful day ensues, the rain and choppy sea in a westerly breeze making visibility from the conning tower poor. Once again, distant destroyers or other enemy units force him under from time to time. The next day offers a brighter prospect. A light westerly breeze is lifting early morning mist over calm waters. At 9.55 am (German time) Rohrbeck observes with sudden excitement a cruiser through his periscope. She has four tall funnels and two masts. She is going to steam straight past him. Keenly, he thumbs through the manual of the enemy fleet kept aboard. 'Probably the *Bellona* or *Boadicea*...' he records in his *Kriegtagesbuch,* or War Diary. Manoeuvring *U 79* to the correct angle for attack, he is only 600 metres from the British ship's starboard side when he gives the order to fire.

CHAPTER SIX
Tuesday 2 October, 1917

The morning mist, which Rohrbeck had observed lifting, enabled HMS *Drake* to obtain a fix of her position: five miles north of Altacarry Head, the north-east corner of Rathlin Island. As planned, they had detached from convoy HH 24 and the Lough Swilly-based escorts an hour before, and left the merchant ships to make their individual way to their discharging ports. Now there was no need to be restricted to the slow speed of the grimy tramp steamers. Labour and noise in the boiler rooms intensified as the cruiser worked up to nineteen knots. Captain Stephen Radcliffe, who had been on the bridge all night as they made landfall and parted from the convoy, ordered the commencement of zigzagging, a recognised tactic against submarines. Every ten minutes the helm would be alternately put over four points to port, then four points to starboard. The officers knew that U-boats were active in these busy north-west approaches to the British Isles. Several ocean-going steamers had been torpedoed in the summer. Lieutenant Alsop posted eleven men along the deck of the cruiser to watch for mines or torpedoes. But the fast zigzagging course ought to ensure the arrival of the ship and the 898 men aboard in the Mersey early that evening.

The torpedo made a white streak as it sped towards the starboard side. Captain Radcliffe saw it. Lieutenant Charles Stewart had the forenoon watch and spotted it, as did Alsop, all within an instant. The helm was immediately put over to starboard, but to no avail. At a range of only 600 metres, Rohrbeck could hardly miss. The torpedo smashed into the *Drake* at a time logged as 9.15 am, directly below the second funnel, blowing a jagged hole in the hull abreast of Number Two Boiler Room.

In the engine room, pulsating and vibrating now that speed had increased, Senior Engineer Lieutenant Bernard Littledale was discussing with Engineer Lieutenant Allen a problem they were encountering with number five port main bearing. There was a tremendous crash and to the officers' astonishment, the whole of the engine room in front of their eyes warped and buckled upwards. The great engines stopped dead for a full 30 seconds, then restarted themselves! Engineer Commander James Barber, the Senior Engineering Officer, hastily appeared. Littledale clambered up above Number Two Boiler Room and peered down into a hatch. It was completely flooded. Realising what had happened, and that steam pressure was dropping rapidly, Barber ordered Littledale to shut off all steam and water connections with it and Number One Boiler Room, forward of it, which reports were saying was damaged and starting to flood. All those in Number One Boiler Room were accounted for, but what had befallen those in Number Two?

William Bridson, an Engine Room Artificer, was standing on top of a grating in Number Two Boiler Room, about ten feet above the stokers, attending to a fan engine when the explosion came. It hurled him sideways against another auxiliary engine, and when he tried to regain his balance, a choking black blast of coal dust swept over him. Instinctively, he groped in the darkness for the ladder up to deck, found it, and emerged gasping into the fresh air, a stoker spilling out of the hatch behind him. But they were the only survivors from Number Two Boiler Room. All Bridson could recall of his comrades' final seconds was 'just a few cries'. The other eighteen men, sixteen stokers and two artificers, lost their lives. They will be returned to later, for they have been the ones sadly rather forgotten over the years – and the source of the biggest misapprehension about the story of the *Drake*…

In Number One Boiler Room, the steam pipes and the main water feed pipe had burst. Barber ordered the fires to be drawn, the boilers shut off and the coal bunker doors closed. These huge vertical sliding doors separated the boiler rooms from the coal bunkers, which ran along the sides of the ship. Of the 43 boilers aboard the cruiser, nineteen were now out of action, but steam pressure was brought back up to normal (275 pounds per square inch) and with the dynamo unaffected and electric power running, the *Drake* was far from helpless – for the time being. The flooding of Number Two Boiler Room had given her a five degree list within five minutes (logged by Rohrbeck as he surveyed what he had done), but water was already also seeping into the adjacent boiler room, Number Three, and the list was increasing. Up on the bridge, it was time for a decision.

At 9.25 am Radcliffe sent a flag signal to the nearby destroyer *Martial* to relay to the Senior Naval Officer, Buncrana: 'Torpedoed. Going to anchor Church Bay. Request instructions.' (Wireless was not used as Radcliffe did not want to risk the submarine learning it had hit a major warship.) The officers made an immediate assessment of their plight, and decided to head for the nearest anchorage, Church Bay, on the opposite side of Rathlin Island, the island's landing point and main settlement. But owing to the explosion, the ship's steam steering engine powering the connection between the wheel and the rudder had failed. A manual emergency system was then turned to, located in a compartment deep down in the stern, above the rudder. The problem to be overcome here was communication from the bridge. The resourceful Commander Harry Morse, second in command to Captain Radcliffe, ordered Crudge, the Master-at-Arms (a Chief Petty Officer responsible for good order on a warship) to set up a semaphore system from the main bridge to the after bridge, whence a chain of messengers conveyed the orders to their sweating comrades manoeuvring the huge wheel set over the rudder. Morse also organised the lowering of the 'collision mat' over the hole made by the torpedo, and, as far as could be judged, this difficult procedure was completed, although a boiler room was already flooded and the water there was causing more problems for its neighbours.

But the initial response to the surprise attack was quick and effective, and as the stricken *Drake* started to push her slow way south towards the east coast of Rathlin, Captain Radcliffe and his colleagues began to reconsider their idea of making for Church Bay to anchor. Belfast with its great repair yards was 50 miles away. Perhaps it could be reached?

*****

Kapitänleutnant Rohrbeck had lingered for a few minutes studying the impact his torpedo had made on the cruiser he wrongly identified as either *Bellona* or *Boadicea* (a four-funnelled pair, too, but much smaller.) The fearful concussion of three depth charges exploding nearby swiftly drew in his periscope, and when he raised it again three-quarters of an hour later, there was no sign of his victim, just a dense cloud of smoke in the direction he assumed she had gone. With another torpedo attack in mind, Rohrbeck followed the smoke. This in fact was a deliberate smokescreen laid by two destroyers speeding across the wake of the *Drake*, which earlier had been firing 'blind' at the estimated position of the U-boat. About eight other destroyers and HM Armed Yacht *Zara*, one of the many peacetime luxury steam yachts requisitioned by the Admiralty, screened the cruiser on either bow. And to add to the confused scene a large fleet oiler rounded Altacarry Head, turning south close astern of the *Drake*. Perhaps this was one of the large steamers logged by Rohrbeck, one of which he tried to attack after having been thwarted by the smokescreen. But he could not get within range (U-boats were very slow underwater) and spent the next four hours avoiding depth charge attacks until he surfaced eventually to the north, nothing in sight.

Explosions, smoke, ships large and small moving hither and thither: the war had come close to Rathlin Island. The grim flotsam and jetsam from sunken ships in the more distant Atlantic waters had of course been washing ashore round the coast, and the islanders had salvaged cheese, cotton, flour, butter, rubber, tobacco and, on occasions, barrels of rum and whisky. Some was even declared to the Customs and Excise! On this morning, 2 October, two island women, Mary Cecil and Mrs Curry, made their way to the top of the cliffs that stretch along the whole north coast of Rathlin, to judge if the incoming tide was bearing any wreckage. They saw far off the convoy with the *Drake* pulling away a few miles ahead of it. A loud explosion carried across the calm water, and the warship temporarily disappeared behind a plume of water. Mary's next recollection was of a lot of gunfire coming from the *Drake* and the convoy changing course to take it through Rathlin Sound instead of round the north of the island. The Cecils lived a few hundred yards from the East Lighthouse on Altacarry Head, and that morning Mary's young brother Dougal, aged about nine, was minding the family's cows. He ran excitedly up to the lighthouse to get a view of the sea, to be greeted by the unforgettable sight of a great four-funnelled warship proceeding close to the land, surrounded by a darting, weaving flotilla of destroyers and with a big tanker following her. The boy's instructions were to herd the cows and he wasn't allowed to leave their fields, so he could only follow the drama from a distance. He watched the warship, listing and belching smoke, pass down the east coast of the island to the right of his vantage point.

Also watching from a low hill a mile or so away was a little girl named Dympna McCurdy. Both these island children would recount their memories in later life. Dympna lived at Croc na Harnan near the east coast, and that morning she had been naughty; in response, she had been told she would be getting no dinner! She took herself off to climb to the top of a low hill, and there beheld to her astonishment the stricken *Drake* and the escorting armada. Dympna ran back to tell her parents, and, her misdeeds forgotten, they hurried off to view the excitement. Cannily, Dympna stayed and helped herself to her dinner after all!

The booming gunfire, as the cruiser fired at a supposed target, had in fact alerted many islanders, John Joe McCurdy, Albert Glass and their colleagues at the limestone quarry near Church Bay heard it, too. Their part in the day's hectic action would soon come. Meanwhile, the boy Dougal and the spellbound watchers above the eastern shore of Rathlin saw the *Drake* start to turn, not to starboard to round Rue Point and enter Church Bay, but to port. What was happening?

Radcliffe, Morse and the others were thinking again about their chances of reaching Belfast. The list to starboard was increasing to almost ten degrees now, and, although steam pressure in the remaining boilers was fine, they were reluctant to proceed at more than about six knots, owing to the colossal strain being imparted on the bulkheads separating the flooded boiler room from its neighbours. Water was flowing all the time into Number Three room, and from there beginning to seep into Number Four. Jellicoe's worries about the bulkheads not being truly watertight, expressed when the ship was new, were being proved right. But as well as all the pipes passing through the bulkheads being liable to seepage, in a riveted ship, any uncaulked plate or loose rivet would yield water through under this pressure. (One can see this happening today in the original riveted gates that hold back the water from the vast Thompson Dry Dock in Belfast, now a tourist stop to view where the *Titanic* was fitted out.) Those in command were not worried about the ship sinking. They felt she could be carefully navigated to safety. But when abeam of Rue Point the optimistic intention of making Belfast was rejected, and the initial plan to anchor in Church Bay decided upon.

Accounts of the day have the *Drake* then – as might be assumed – turn to starboard, but in fact she turned to port initially, as Dougal Cecil recalled all those years later, and steamed in a huge, slow circle, crossing back over her track and heading straight into Rathlin Sound about half a mile south of Rue Point. The reason for this was probably to minimise the pressure on the straining bulkheads by making the final starboard turn into Church Bay 90 degrees rather than the full 180 degrees it would have been had she not come round in a circle.

But the *Drake* was becoming increasingly hard to manoeuvre. The orders were still being conveyed by semaphore and then a relay of voices to the hot confines of the stern steering post, but she was not steering straight, lurching and yawing from side to side. From her foremast now flew the international signal 'Not Under Command'. Her steam siren to warn other vessels was out of action. It was now about 10.30 am. The warships screening *Drake* could dodge around quickly, but the tramp steamers from convoy HH 24 now labouring towards her through the Sound had to beware. The first three of them passed safely on the mainland side of her. Next to assess the situation was Captain Francis Theaker, a 48 year-old skipper from Grimsby, as he brought the *Mendip Range* past Church Bay on his port side, Ballycastle to starboard. He saw through his binoculars the 'Not Under Command' signal, and decided the struggling warship was going to cross his bows. If she was not under command, he reasoned, she was not going to be able to change course significantly.

Back at the stern of the *Mendip Range* a group of the crew were gathered on the platform housing the defensive gun, among them one of the ship's two apprentices, seventeen year old Cyril Potts from Doncaster. He and his shipmates could not help stopping what they were instructed to do, watch for periscopes and mines, and they gazed over at the approaching wounded giant…

CHAPTER SEVEN
'You'll Catch Her on the Turn!'

Second Officer John McDowell, though off duty, had appeared on the bridge wing of the *Mendip Range*, trying to judge with Captain Theaker, Chief Officer Fred Houlden and Third Officer Thomas Lowe what was happening. Danger was around them, above and below the waves, as they steamed eastwards through Rathlin Sound. The *Drake* was surely going to cross their bows. Those in charge must have decided to beach her on the long sands visible at Ballycastle.

The crew up on the gun platform all seemed to call out together, Potts later recounted: 'She's turning, there's going to be a collision!' But it was John Gemmell, the Chief Gunner, who remembered the Yorkshire apprentice's hobby – photography. 'Look out, you'll catch her on the turn!' The *Drake* was indeed making a big turn to starboard, the side to which she was listing, as she made for Church Bay. Now she was not going to cross their bows. Potts scurried along the deck and down to his cabin. When he emerged again, clutching his treasured Cameo camera, the cruiser was noticeably nearer, just about 400 or 500 metres away. A collision indeed seemed inevitable. He pushed the lens back as far as it would go, setting the bellows camera to infinity, and took two photographs a short interval apart.

The listing, smoking *Drake* loomed larger, figures now visible waving their arms, gesticulating frantically, frustrated that the steam power to the siren had failed. Captain Theaker ordered the helmsman to swing hard to port, then ordered him again – hard to starboard! The *Drake* kept coming nearer. As a last hope, Theaker rang the engine room telegraph for the engines to be put full astern. It clanged, and three blasts on the tramp steamer's siren rang out. It was to no avail. At 10.37 am the concave, ram-shaped bow of the warship penetrated the *Mendip Range* in Number Two hold, just forward of the bridge, laden with flour in bags. Within a few minutes, as sodden bags started floating out, it was obvious the steamer was taking on so much water she was going to sink, so course was set for the sandy expanse of beach between Ballycastle and Fair Head that they had at first thought the

Drake was making for. Less than an hour later, the *Mendip Range* was safely beached.

Little did Cyril Potts think that his 'devotion to the photographic art' would make the national press four years later, when a protracted legal dispute over the damage to his ship reached its conclusion. But for now he and his shipmates (and the precious film in his camera) were all safe. A few minutes after the *Mendip Range* crunched into the sand, though, another explosion echoed across Rathlin Sound. One of Rohrbeck's mines had claimed a victim.

By this time, all work in the limestone quarry to the west of Church Bay had stopped. The labourers had a panoramic view of the action on a day they were always to recall. John Joe McCurdy, Albert Glass and their workmates had witnessed the collision between the *Drake* and the *Mendip Range* and the two ships slowly disengaging. The *Drake* was lumbering on towards Church Bay, when, just before 11.30 am, came the big explosion away to the men's right. To their astonishment, the entire forward part of a warship was thrown bodily into the air. It splashed back into the water and floated for a time, bow upwards, they recounted decades later, before disappearing. Snapped in two, the rest of the ship, which turned out to be the destroyer HMS *Brisk*, drifted helplessly. It was one of Rohrbeck's string of mines laid to the south of Bull Point on 29 September which had done the damage, but until the British and German archives were examined in detail in the 1990s, it had been thought *U 79* or another U-boat might have entered Rathlin Sound with the dispersing convoy and its escorts in search of further prey. However, the logs of HMS *Martin*, HMS *Wolf* and the armed yacht *Zara* all attributed the explosion to a mine at the time. These three units were among those which kept close to the *Drake* during her final hours. The *Brisk* was one of the Lough Swilly-based destroyers which was escorting the convoy on its transit of Rathlin Sound. (Earlier in the year, she had rescued over 200 survivors of a troopship sunk in a collision off the Isle of Wight.) Among the number was a steamer named *Lugano* which had loaded steel, alcohol and bales of cotton in Norfolk, Virginia, before assembling in Hampton Roads and setting off in HH 24.

The *Brisk* was just ahead of the *Lugano* and on the Rathlin side of her when the merchantman's crew saw her go up. A few minutes later, they too were rocked by a huge detonation – another of Rohrbeck's mines.

The quarrymen, and the islanders watching all this in amazement from the cliffs and the settlement at Church Bay, could see the *Drake* finally reaching her intended sanctuary a few hundred yards offshore at just about the same time the *Lugano* was sinking from view beneath the waves four miles to the west. Near her, the mutilated silhouette of the *Brisk* was being approached by two of the many armed trawlers on hire to the Admiralty, *Seaton* and *Vale of Lennox*. There might have been another twenty ships in Rathlin Sound. Was there ever a scene like it round the Irish coast?

The quarry workers felt they had to do something to help. They could not just gaze at this spectacle unfolding. A small boat had set out to row across to the *Drake* but turned back when they were hailed by a warship and told the cruiser might blow up. Still determined to be of use, the island men then made for the lifeboats visible coming from the sinking *Lugano* and the survivors eventually rowed themselves ashore not far from the quarry. About 50 crew from the *Lugano* landed on the island, the only seamen out of well over 1,000 from the four casualties of this momentous day actually to set foot on Rathlin.

All the crew of the *Lugano* had got off safely, but the *Brisk*, commanded by Lieutenant R C Smith, incurred 31 deaths and 12 wounded, one of whom, Able Seaman Brooke, from Exeter, died later in hospital. The wounded, 11 ratings and Sub-Lieutenant Sims, were transferred to the *Vale of Lennox* and the *Seaton* took the severed stern section in tow for Derry within ten minutes of the explosion. In command of the *Seaton* was Lieutenant John Whitfield RNR, who was mentioned in despatches for this operation in mined and hazardous waters, and one the previous January when he had rescued some of the survivors from the gold ship *Laurentic*, also mined at the mouth of Lough Swilly. Ten hours later, the *Brisk* was tied up at Derry and the crew accommodated in the Sailors' Home.

These young officers had eventful wars. Incident after incident was occurring in the north-west approaches, although never so concentrated into one morning like 2 October 1917. Another RNR Lieutenant, G R Parry, commanded the elderly four-funnelled destroyer *Wolf* and his detailed report in response to the request of the Commodore at his base, Larne, provides a succinct but graphic source for these eventful hours. He is close to Torr Head in company with the *Zara* when he first hears the heavy firing after the *Drake* is hit: he proceeds north, falling in with the action: stays on the port quarter of the cruiser until just before the collision, and returns then to Torr Head to make a visual signal to the look-out station up on the promontory. Just after steaming back into Rathlin Sound, Parry sees the *Brisk* blown in two. That could have been the *Wolf*. Rathlin Sound is obviously mined, so he is ordered by the *Zara* and *Martin*, which are by now near the anchored *Drake*, to stop all shipping entering Rathlin Sound from the south. The Belfast steam coaster *Castledobbs* is hailed near Torr Head, and later the Liverpool to Derry passenger steamer *Comic* is turned and re-directed to Belfast. The passengers must have had to continue their journey by train. (Much alarm was caused throughout these years to Irish Sea passengers, culminating late in the war on 10 October 1918, when the *Leinster* actually was torpedoed with the loss of some 500 lives, an act which delayed talks about an Armistice.) If the passengers had not already heard word of what had happened, they were able on Saturday next, 6 October, to read a brief report of the sinking of the *Drake* in the 'Londonderry Sentinel', the Admiralty having made a terse official announcement the day before: '...the ship was torpedoed off the north coast of Ireland, reached harbour, but sank in shallow water...'

CHAPTER EIGHT
In Shallow Water: The Final Anchorage

Only about fifteen feet of water lay under the keel of the *Drake* when her anchors rattled down in Church Bay at 11.46 am. She was just about 400 metres from the shore, and soundings showed a depth of about 43 feet, with the ship drawing 28 feet. The weather was calm and overcast, with a slight south-westerly breeze and occasional light rain. At the inquiry, Captain Radcliffe was asked why he did not run the ship aground in Church Bay. His reasoned reply was that they were aware of a steeply shelving bottom, and therefore he felt that if the bow was aground and the stern afloat, there would be a greater risk of her capsizing, because the shock of taking the ground might cause the collapse of the stressed bulkheads and a roll over to starboard. It is intriguing to speculate what might have been the outcome had the *Drake* continued across Rathlin Sound to Ballycastle strand and been driven on to the flatter sands, as the *Mendip Range* was. This option never seems to have been discussed by those on the bridge of the *Drake*, and is not put forward by those presiding over the inquiry. Undoubtedly, Radcliffe and his officers did not think the ship would sink until shortly before she did capsize, and were intent on taking her to a sheltered anchorage where tugs would shortly arrive to take her to a repair yard. In fact, a wireless message at twelve noon from the Senior Naval Officer in Larne assured Radcliffe that the tug *Flying Cormorant* was coming from Lough Swilly and two had been despatched from Belfast. Shortly afterwards, further news was transmitted that another tug, the Belfast Harbour Commissioners' *Musgrave*, and one from Ardrossan in Ayrshire were also hastening to Rathlin. The situation was in hand, it seemed.

Commander Harry Morse, the Second in Command, was probably aware of the large notice in bold brass letters in Osborne Naval College on the Isle of Wight: 'There Is Nothing The Navy Cannot Do.' Having already that morning organised the semaphore and verbal relaying of steering orders and supervised the lowering of the collision mat, Morse now took charge of a pressing need: feeding nearly 900 men.

Because of the extreme circumstances, the complex Navy system of catering in a great many separate messes aboard was overridden. Everyone was ordered to the upper deck on the port side – counteracting the list – where tinned meat was issued and bread and jam passed round, washed down by gallons of tea. (No record exists of whether the men were issued with their daily tot of rum at noon!) Commander Morse had been torpedoed previously while serving on HMS *Dublin* in the Adriatic and was to go on to win the DSO 'for distinguished services under fire on several occasions.' He is one of three officers particularly singled out for praise in Radcliffe's official report – although the ship's company as a whole is commended – the others being Engineer Commander Barber and Senior Engineer Littledale. Barber, when addressing the investigators at Devonport, does make highly technical criticisms of the ship's pumping arrangements, but these were not taken up by the Court in its findings.

So, with the pumps trying as best they could to cope, and the tilt on the deck steepening, the *Drake* summoned alongside her the destroyer *Martin* and began transferring men. It was still hoped to keep some men aboard to await the tugs, but as the list had increased to eighteen degrees, Radcliffe decided to abandon her. What was causing the huge ship to lean ever more steeply to starboard? The officers felt sure the pressure of water in the flooded boiler rooms was starting the collapse of the longitudinal, or length-wise, bulkheads which separated the boiler rooms from the coal bunkers between them and the ship's side. These were huge vertical steel doors raised and lowered by chain and pulley mechanisms. As even they failed, the flooding spread outwards to the starboard side of the ship and naturally increased the angle of her plight. Soon the *Martin* was joined in the evacuation by another destroyer the *Gossamer* and the sloop *Delphinium*. After absorbing as many men as she could, the *Martin* cast off from the side of the *Drake* and went alongside the armed yacht *Zara*, transferring 250 men to her. The *Zara*, which was only 422 gross tons and must have been very crowded, made for Belfast, while the *Martin* was ordered to Buncrana, although she went east via Rue Point and rounded the island, no doubt owing to the threat of the mines which had been struck by the *Brisk* and *Lugano*, and then north of Inishtrahull rather than between the island and the Donegal mainland, again with the mining of Inishtrahull Sound in mind.

Captain Stephen Radcliffe was the last to leave his ship. He stepped aboard the *Delphinium*, ordering her CO to anchor nearby to await the tugs. His report concludes:

> …nobody except the dead remained on board the *Drake* when I left her for the *Delphinium*: the mess decks, boiler rooms, engine rooms had all been searched and reported clear. Ship was abandoned at 2.05 p.m. I ordered the *Delphinium* to anchor close to the *Drake* intending to go back aboard as soon as the salvage plant arrived, but the list rapidly increased and the ship capsized at 2.35 p.m., lying over on her beam ends with part of the port side out of the water. After this occurred, I ordered *Delphinium* to proceed to Buncrana.

Nearly 900 men were safely taken off the *Drake*. It is clear that the organisation, seamanship and discipline were all first class. But the weather was favourable, too, and so was the length of time – just – that the threatened bulkheads stood firm below. It is instructive to contrast a dreadful event which occurred a year later just twenty miles to the north, off the Scottish island of Islay, when the inward-bound troopship *Otranto*, damaged in a collision with the *Kashmir*, had to be abandoned in bad weather as she drifted towards the shore. The destroyer HMS *Mouncey*, another of the Buncrana force, took off no fewer than 596 men as she bobbed up and down alongside the *Otranto*, smashing into her sides, but many more were killed or injured as they leapt for her decks below.

With an immense, prolonged, titanic rumble the *Drake*, all 14,000 tons of her, rolled over and sank. A towering cloud of smoke and steam rose into the autumn sky as a small tsunami rippled outwards from the disturbed calmness of Church Bay. Radcliffe's responsibility had ended; he had done all he could and was now on his way to Buncrana Naval Base to prepare his report. The Navy would soon find a fresh post for him. But the giant presence of the crippled ship on their doorstep meant Church Bay would never be the same for the islanders: nearly a century later everyone arriving and leaving passes the 'Drake Buoy' and it is one of the most popular dive sites round the coasts. But the immediate reaction was awe – and fear. Still obediently minding the cows near the East Lighthouse on Altacarry Head, Dougal Cecil was sitting on the hill near his house when he witnessed the *Drake* capsize, recalling forever the sound like thunder and the soaring cloud as her boiler fires were quenched by the inrush of cold salt water.

At the stone quay in Church Bay, the island's landing place, a Naval motor launch had arrived to warn the residents that there was a danger the cruiser's magazines might explode! Consequently, the children of the island school a few hundred metres away were sent home. Some of the residents took refuge on the far side of Rathlin, and young Dougal recalled not being able to sleep that night as there had been so much talk among the grown-ups that the *Drake* might blow up. Micky Joe Anderson, again decades later, remembered how he and some others had crossed to Ballycastle that morning, but when they attempted to return in the afternoon, they were prevented by one of the Naval vessels. Later, they were allowed to leave but were warned not to approach the sunken ship. Micky Joe recalled that when they had rowed to the entrance to Church Bay, their progress was impeded by all the wreckage floating there. Paddy Anderson also remembered that 'you could have walked out on the bay on all the wreckage', including hundreds of bales of cotton which had been part of the cargo of the *Lugano*. Among the items well worth salvaging was one of the lifeboats of the *Drake*, which the islanders towed into their harbour and pulled up on the sand beside the boathouse (nowadays the Visitors' Centre, with displays about this epic day). It was later acquired by the Murray family of Waterfoot, Co Antrim, and used in their salvage business around Rathlin and elsewhere. Another lifeboat came into the ownership of Ballycastle man John Coll, who fitted her out with a simple lugsail that could be raised and dipped plus a motor, and used her for fishing.

One local man was among the crew of the *Drake*. He was Patrick Morrison, of Union Street, Ballycastle, and the legend was that he was called on deck to see his home town come into view, thus saving his life when the torpedo struck! Patrick died in 1937, and in a sadder echo of the *Drake,* his nephew Patrick Duffin lost his life in 1941 in the disastrous sinking by Japanese planes of the battle-cruiser HMS *Repulse*. Patrick Morrison is buried in Ballycastle, and on the same gravestone, his nephew is commemorated.

Next day, fear of explosion had receded and the islanders ventured out to the wreck. It is interesting to speculate for how long this would be forbidden in our security and health-and-safety conscious times! The whole island would probably be evacuated. Then, the authorities simply seem to have left the *Drake*, her story over as far as they were concerned. Bill Curry recalled that as they rowed round the wreck, they could see brasswork still shining under the water. Oil and air continued to bubble to the surface (no-one worried about pollution in 1917, there were too many more momentous things happening) and the odd bit of wreckage was still bobbing up. Paddy Anderson and his colleagues rowed farther out that day into the Sound to collect bags of flour from the *Mendip Range* which had washed out of the gash in her side made by the bow of the *Drake*. They found to their delight that bags not contaminated by oil were still useable, as the seawater had only penetrated an inch or so and formed a protective skin over good, dry American flour!

So the *Drake* was to lie in Church Bay for ever more, part of the hull visible until about 1929, like a colossal stranded whale. Eighteen bodies lay entombed under the toppled hull. She did not blow up, and young Dougal Cecil soon resumed his untroubled slumbers. The survivors were dispersed in Belfast and Derry, never to sail together as a crew again. The officers and crew who landed at Derry were cared for and entertained at Ebrington Barracks by a battalion of the Royal Inniskilling Fusiliers, and to this day the Regimental Museum in Enniskillen holds the silver cup presented in thanks to the officers' mess, and a silver challenge shield for billiards presented to the Sergeants' Mess. On their departure, the crew were played to the railway station by the band and pipers of the battalion. Captain Radcliffe later wrote to the CO of the Battalion, thanking him 'for the perfectly wonderful reception which you accorded me and the officers and men of the *Drake*'. (Sadly, Lieutenant Charles Stewart, who had initially spotted the torpedo, was to be torpedoed again two months later in HMS *Arbutus*, and this time did not survive.)

Meanwhile, the German submariner who caused it all, Kapitänleutnant Otto Rohrbeck, was heading northwards. By the next day he was 120 miles away, still intent on attacks. The autumn weather now setting in was against him. Mist, rain and a heavy swell kept him mostly submerged for a couple of days. On Friday, 5 October, with his engines giving problems, and the weather no better, he logs 'I decide to return to home port.' But there was yet to be one fatal postscript to his mission.

It will be recalled that a few days before the engagement with the *Drake*, Rohrbeck had laid mines off Islay, to the north of Rathlin. He was safely back in the U-boat base in Brunsbüttel when the

Admiralty trawler *Earl Lennox* struck one and immediately sank. It was 23 October, and the trawler was escorting an ammunition carrier southwards towards the Clyde. She had been hired, like hundreds of others, from owners in Grimsby in April 1915 and armed with a six-pounder gun. Although the location is imprecise, and the wreck has not been found, they seem to have been off the southern end of the Sound of Islay, which separates Islay and Jura, when at 1.00 pm, a big explosion under the bows fatally holed her. Captain Taylor and a seaman had been watching for mines and torpedoes but saw nothing, Rohrbeck's mines being placed just below the surface, as described earlier. Seven of the crew of the *Earl Lennox*, all Royal Naval Reserve, lost their lives.

Kapitänleutnant Rohrbeck and the Germans would certainly have known of their success in sinking the *Drake*, which was admitted in the British press, but probably not the mines' victims, *Brisk*, *Lugano* and *Earl Lennox*. Rohrbeck did not go to sea again, but was appointed chief of the Second U-boat Flotilla, finally being discharged from the Imperial Germany Navy in April 1919.

The man his course fatefully crossed, Captain Radcliffe, next commanded a similar cruiser, the *Achilles*, and then the battleship *Superb*, in which the C in C, Mediterranean Fleet, Admiral Gough-Calthorpe, flew his flag. The ship was at Constantinople at the time of its occupation by the Allies, the armistice with Turkey coming shortly before the cessation of the fighting in the west. More than four years of world war on an unparalleled scale was ending. By no means everything has since been examined by archivists and historians. Nearly a century later, many incidents and stories of the survivors and the dead still need to be illuminated…

CHAPTER NINE

'Nobody Except the Dead Remained...': The Black Squad

The strangest and most regrettable aspect of the *Drake* saga is how the eighteen fatalities have been almost forgotten. It has usually been assumed, and repeated in print, that the bodies were removed after the event, but this cannot be true. There are no graves anywhere. The Commonwealth War Graves Commission lists brief details of the men in its database, recording in each case 'killed in action with submarine, North Channel, 2 October 1917', but there are no War Graves on Rathlin or elsewhere. The inescapable fact is that they were never taken off the ship, either in the immediate aftermath or later. It would have been an impossibly difficult task, with their flooded Number Two Boiler Room lying on the submerged starboard side and the whole weight and depth of the capsized ship on top of it. But this raises a question sometimes asked: should the wreck of the *Drake* not be protected as a War Grave?

Before considering this, it is worth pausing and looking at the life of a Royal Navy stoker, not the type of man to have attracted much historical attention, although the coal-fired Navy required many thousands of them. The *Drake* alone had some 300, comprising the ranks of Stoker, Stoker First Class, Leading Stoker, Chief Stoker and, most senior, Petty Officer Stoker. This should give a hint that there was much more to the job than shovelling coal into a fiery furnace. In fact, a great deal of training and experience were needed besides sheer stamina. The fires had to be kept fed and spread to the optimum level and the 'clinker' removed at well-judged intervals by means of a thick seven-foot long rod called a 'slice'. The most junior stokers would be toiling as 'trimmers', hauling the coal from the bunkers along the ship's side in a tub on rails or a heavy iron bucket called a 'skid', while more senior comrades would keep an eye on the equal movement of coal to ensure the ship stayed on an even keel. The more senior ranks would also be responsible for steam pressure and water pressure, furnace fans, the state of the exhaust gases and the many other tasks required for the efficient operation of a huge steam engine. All ranks were trained in boiler mechanics and the workings of steam-powered machinery. To do their job at the best of times was demanding; to do it in rough seas or very hot climatic conditions was even more so; to do it under shellfire with the ship demanding maximum speed is barely imaginable. At the Battle of the Falklands in 1914 furniture was even broken up for fuel when HMS *Kent* ran low on coal as her Captain pushed the engine room for an extra knot during, as he termed it, 'a devilish good scrap'. And, as the story of the *Drake* reveals, the stokers were the most vulnerable to the new menace of U-boat attack.

A strange phenomenon often happens when researchers are on a quest through historical records: crucial material seems to find them, rather than the other way round. This mysterious force of attraction can be credited now with the appearance of the 1920s book 'A Stoker's Log' in a dealer's catalogue just when authentic details of a stoker's life on a ship like the *Drake* were most required! The obscure author of this very well-written account of his wartime career is Henry Vincent, who volunteered to be a stoker in 1915 ('I want to join the Royal Navy!' 'What do you want to join as, an Admiral?' I told him my aim was not quite so high...') After serving on cruisers in West Africa and the North Sea, he is demobbed a month after the Armistice and the book concludes with him stepping out on a cold afternoon towards Harwich railway station and civilian life again, the long grey shapes of the warships growing indistinct behind him in the December dusk. We learn precisely nothing about who he is, and his life before and after the Royal Navy. Perhaps the only thing we can be sure about Henry Vincent is that his name was not Henry Vincent! There seems every chance this is a nom-de-plume. But he says he never felt more alive than when serving, and has a clear desire to pay tribute to the 'Black Squad':

> ...I found the stoker was not the abandoned reprobate that popular view often makes him out to be...it is true, stokers are looked upon as a lower order of seafarer. They are necessary, but they are not sailors...they have all the vices of seamen, but none of the virtues. This is the popular view...

He goes on to quote a scurrilous tale of the day that it was (naturally) a stoker who attempted to steal the lifebelt of the wireless operator of the *Titanic* as he tapped out the distress calls. But the author hopes that on finishing the book, the reader will take a kindlier view of 'these large-handed and large-hearted fellows, the grimy clinker-knockers...'

> ...I found that the worst looking ruffians were often the most generous and reliable shipmates... the stokers had their own standards of conduct, and if their ideals were not such as would meet with unqualified support at a clergy conference, I can at all event say that they upheld their standards in all circumstances... with them it was no sort of fault to purloin a piece of soap, but the theft of a man's tot of rum was considered a misdemeanour so gross I do not think a person could be found to commit such an act...

While finding this rare book fortuitously provided an insight into the wartime life on a coal-fired cruiser, the endless labyrinths of the internet, and the many sites dedicated to family history, have yielded the life story of a stoker who was actually aboard the *Drake* on 2 October 1917 and survived. But his naval career did not have a contented ending like Henry Vincent.

William Wheelhouse was born in the St Paul's area of inner-city Sheffield in 1890. His mother, losing her husband to illness at an early age, struggled to raise her four sons, of whom William was the youngest. He attended Sheffield District Boys Charity School, then began work in one of Sheffield's famous steel mills. Noted in his Naval records are two scars on his shoulder, perhaps the result of burns suffered there. Short and stocky, and familiar with hard physical labour, William joined the Royal Navy aged twenty in 1910, training at the shore establishment *Victory II* and then aboard the old battleship *Renown*.

Henry Vincent summed up the duties they had to qualify in: 'stoker, greaser, bricklayer, fireman and sweep' (the bricklaying being firebricks laid in furnace fireboxes). He also remarks on the assortment of men who join up: '...just all sorts, factory hands, shop assistants, gas stokers, puddlers, locomotive drivers, most of them used to hard labour, but some of them rather difficult subjects, with views of their own about naval discipline...'.

William's first ship was the new cruiser *Weymouth* which was deployed at Constantinople at the time of serious tension between Greece and Turkey, some of the ship's company being landed as an armed guard at the British Embassy. He joined the *Drake* when the threat of war resulted in her being re-commissioned in the summer of 1914, and was aboard for the escort of the *Olympic* and the voyage round the North Cape to Archangel with the *Mantua*. His service records pronounce his ability 'superior' and he became an Acting Leading Stoker, then on 1 December 1916 was promoted to Leading Stoker. By this time as we have seen the ship was on the Navy's North America and West Indies stations, based in Bermuda. So he had seen much more of the world than he would have done had he stayed in the Sheffield steelworks.

After the attack off Rathlin which he survived, he may perhaps have been among the company of stokers praised by Captain Radcliffe in his official report: 'The third steaming watch of stokers carried on as if nothing had happened and continued in the same calm manner.'

William Wheelhouse's next posting was to the destroyer HMS *Pincher*, part of the Second Destroyer Flotilla at Buncrana, which had been so involved on 2 October. She was commanded by 28 year-old Lieutenant Patrick W R Weir. Further promotion to Petty Office Stoker came on 1 March 1918. Two months later, the *Pincher* was allocated to the Fourth Destroyer Flotilla, based at Devonport.

On 24 July 1918, the *Pincher* and another destroyer, the *Scorpion*, were escorting the Royal Fleet Auxiliary tanker *War Hostage* from Devonport to a Scottish destination. Around 3.30 am, in fog, the *Pincher* crashed on to the Seven Stones Reef off Land's End. (Lieutenant Weir was later reprimanded by the Admiralty for the failings of his navigation.) The warship was a complete wreck and thirteen of the crew, nine of them stokers, were lost. William Wheelhouse was among them. His body was washed up some days later at Gwithian, at the east end of St Ives Bay and near Godrevy Lighthouse. Today, in the quiet local churchyard, his grave is still cared for by the Commonwealth War Graves Commission.

Of course, every man aboard the *Drake* had his own story, like young Philip Danby Collin, a boy from a prosperous family of gentleman farmers in Suffolk, who joined the Navy during the war to escape his tyrannical father!

The melancholy, but comforting, thought of the last resting place of William Wheelhouse brings us back to his shipmates who died on the *Drake* and have no grave but the wreck. The list taken from the database of the Commonwealth War Graves Commission is appended to this narrative. It will be seen there were sixteen stokers of different ranks, the most senior being Petty Officer Stoker Robert O'Brien, aged 33, of Strand Street, Skerries, Co Dublin. Each boiler room had a Petty Officer Stoker overseeing each watch. Also lost were two Engine Room Artificers, Tynesider James Patterson, 26, and Isle of Wight man Adolphus Stark, 37. Engine Room Artificers were highly skilled men, time-served tradesmen such as fitter and turner, coppersmith, boilermaker or engine smith and were in charge of all engine and boiler-room machinery. They were also capable of manufacturing replacement parts aboard, to a high standard. It has already been mentioned that a third of a coal-burning cruiser's crew was made up of stoker ranks, and on a destroyer this proportion was even higher, speed being the main priority. When the *Brisk* hit the mine, the stokers again suffered the most casualties, and two of the three War Graves in the City Cemetery, Derry, are of stokers.

So, on the *Drake*, eighteen men of the twenty in Boiler Room Two lost their lives. Engine Room Artificer William Henry Leece Bridson, as we have seen, escaped out of the stokehold hatch (and, nothing daunted, returned to work in Boiler Room Three, an act mentioned by Radcliffe in his report), followed, he said, by an unnamed stoker. All Bridson recalled was 'just a few cries'. And that is just about all the attention those who died, no doubt by drowning in the sudden flooding, get in the Captain's report or the proceedings of the Devonport Court Martial. Their names do appear on the great Naval Memorials at Chatham, Plymouth and Portsmouth. It does have to be asked though: under the terms of the Protection of Military Remains Act, 1986, is the *Drake* site protected from disturbance?

Military aircraft wrecks are automatically designated. Some shipwrecks are designated as 'controlled sites', on which diving is banned. All other vessels that meet the criteria are subject, since more recent statutes, to a rolling programme of assessment and those which meet the criteria will be designated as 'protected places', which is given to mean that diving is allowed, but divers must follow the rule of: look, but do not touch... There are currently 55 such sites, but the *Drake* is not one. Perhaps one day it will be.

In the comprehensive survey of the wreck undertaken in 2006 by Wessex Archaeology on behalf of the Northern Ireland Environment Agency, Assessment Point 7.1.4 states:

> taking into account the controlled site status of other armoured cruisers such as HMS *Hampshire* and HMS *Natal*, and the fact that HMS *Drake* may contain eighteen bodies in the area of boiler room two, the designation of the wreck under the Protection of Military Remains Act, 1986, cannot be discounted...

Point 7.1.5 adds: 'further research is required to ascertain whether salvage operations retrieved the dead following the loss of H.M.S. *Drake* and to further assess its suitability for protection under the Act'. Surely, once it has been found that the Commonwealth War Graves Commission has no place of burial for these men, no further research is called for. The sixteen stokers and two Artificers who died at their posts were never retrieved.

In the City Cemetery, Derry, though, can easily be found three War Graves of men from the *Brisk*, named Owens, Pawley and Withey. It would seem certain that the majority of the casualties happened in the fore part of the ship, which sank in Rathlin Sound, and were never recovered. The 'Londonderry Sentinel' fully recorded the solemn funerals – except for the name of the ship, owing to censorship:

> ...at the head of the procession marched the firing party of the 3rd Inniskillings. Then came a gun-carriage and two Army Service Corps wagons, each containing a coffin draped in Union Jacks, on which were placed numerous floral tributes. Then came a detachment of Inniskillings, men of deceased's ship under four officers, representatives from other naval units, marines, French naval seamen and the city police...

Among the 'other naval units' were surely men from the *Drake* herself, the main casualty of 2 October 1917 – but not the most costly, it must be remembered, in terms of lives.

CHAPTER TEN

The Neptune Steam Navigation Co Vs Captain Stephen Herbert Radcliffe

When we left the *Mendip Range*, Captain Theaker had beached her safely on Ballycastle strand, midway between the mouth of the Margy River and the Pans Rocks towards Fair Head. There she lay for almost a month while temporary repairs were carried out, ammunition on board having been speedily removed by Admiralty trawlers which came alongside at high tide. No-one had been injured in the collision, and some of the crew including Cyril Potts the young photographer, were sent home, looked after by the Shipwrecked Fishermen and Mariners' Society. During her unscheduled stay another stoker became an indirect victim of the events. He was a Swede named Gustav Petersson, who had developed a high temperature as the ship crossed the Atlantic, and was removed to Ballycastle hospital, where he sadly died of consumption. Petersson's pathetically few items of clothing were ordered to be burnt, and his passport and pocket book were forwarded to the Swedish consulate in Belfast.

Hugh Boyd, a well-known Ballycastle figure and keen local historian, recalled that some of the cargo washed ashore and was put to good use, including condensed milk as well as the flour the islanders were keen on, too. He was aboard the ship the day she was towed off, 4 November. Course was set for Glasgow and a repair yard, but when abeam of Torr Head, she began to leak again and was beached in Red Bay. Finally, four days later, the *Mendip Range* was successfully towed to the Clyde.

But that was far from the end of the story of the collision. In fact, the court cases the owners brought for damages took up a great deal more time than the Admiralty Court Martial in Devonport which inquired into the actual loss of the *Drake*. It was 1921 before a final appeal went to the House of Lords when the apprentice with the camera, Cyril Potts, had his brief moment of fame in the newspapers as he received a lofty rebuke from one of the five Law Lords hearing the case, Lord Atkinson: though detailed to watch for mines and torpedoes, he had gone below for his camera. His ship was in danger; but two very useful photographs were the result and formed part of the evidence. That had to be admitted. Very frustratingly, Potts' views of the approaching *Drake* now seem lost. Although the proceedings of the case survive, the photographs are no longer with them. But the legal clash is a fascinating one, resting as it does on a nice point of nautical law that even the expert assessors needed at the hearings could not agree on: was or was not Captain Theaker of the *Mendip Range* justified in thinking that the 'Not Under Command' signal of two black balls flying from the cruiser's forestay meant she would largely maintain her course across his bow? In short, was she under command or not?

On first impressions, knowing the desperate plight of the *Drake* it seems somehow unsporting, for want of a better word, for her Captain to be sued at all (following an Admiralty inquiry, the Captain would by legal custom be the one arraigned at any subsequent Court proceedings.) Captain Radcliffe had to take passage home from Malta for the affair, and no doubt his officers who re-assembled at the High Court of Justice – except the late Lieutenant Stewart – had to be summoned from various postings. Surely the incident was just a clear example of 'the fog of war'?

But the Neptune Steam Navigation Company of West Hartlepool did not see it that way. They felt they had a strong case in maritime law. This firm since 1910 had been part of the growing Furness, Withy & Co shipping empire, which at the time of the collision controlled well over 200 ships and was well on its way to becoming one of Britain's major companies. No doubt a smaller concern could not have entertained thoughts of fighting a legal case, certainly not through an appeal and ultimately to the House of Lords.

The case opened in January 1919 before the Hon Mr Justice Roche, assisted by Rear-Admiral G R Mansell and Captain A W Clarke, both Elder Brethren of Trinity House, the lighthouse and pilotage authority, as nautical assessors. All Captain Theaker and his three officers, Houlden, McDowell and Lowe could do was reiterate the firm belief they shared at the time that the *Drake*, by flying a 'Not Under Command' signal, would not be making any significant alteration to her westwards course. By going to port, they judged they would avoid the *Drake* and pass between Rue Point, Rathlin, and the stricken warship. Witnesses called by the defendant were the Navigating Officer, Alison, Lieutenant-Commander Back, Engineer Commander Barber and Lieutenant Reed, who had been commanding HMS *Martin*. For their part, they stated that the cruiser was damaged and making water and was simply intent on making for a safe anchorage. Had the *Mendip Range* simply gone to starboard, as the *Drake* turned into Church Bay, rather than to port, she would have passed beyond their stern on the mainland side of Rathlin Sound.

The judgment therefore rested on the expert assessors' interpretation of the Regulations for Preventing Collisions at Sea, 1897. Regarding a 'Not Under Command' signal, these stated that it should be flown 'if a vessel is not absolutely helpless, but unable to make the manoeuvres she would be reasonably expected to make'. The assessors could not agree with each other, one finding for the tramp steamer's claim, one against. The Hon Mr Justice Roche, admitting he found himself now in a difficult position, but exercising the wisdom of Solomon, found that neither vessel was to blame!

The Neptune Steam Navigation Company appealed; the court upheld the original verdict. The final recourse was to the Lords. Here Mr Justice Roche's verdict was again sustained, but only by a three to two majority among the five Law Lords sitting in judgement.

This was when Cyril Potts, the budding photographer, had his fifteen minutes of fame:

> Lord Atkinson said the story of the apprentice was most extraordinary. If it were true it was not to be wondered at that many ships were lost. The *Mendip Range* carried a gun or guns, presumably to protect herself against hostile attack by submarines among other craft. Potts, the apprentice, belonged to the crew of one of the guns. His business apparently was to watch for submarines and presumably to help to fire on them if they appeared. He himself stated in evidence that he was supposed to be looking after submarines… neither the demands of duty nor the danger of being torpedoed and sunk by one of the submarines he was employed to shoot at, said Lord Atkinson, could chill this apprentice's devotion to the photographic art. The only effect of the danger upon him was to make him think it would be interesting to take a snapshot of the torpedoed cruiser coming round. He took

his photographs, and the result was the enlargements produced in this case.

Lord Atkinson's rebuke does not seem absolutely unkind, though we obviously do not know the precise tone of his voice! Is it possible there was a twinkle in the eye of the eminent 77 year-old Law Lord, who at one time had been MP for North Londonderry, and whose personality was said to be 'kindly, though unconventional'?

What happened to these photographs? Alas, they seem to have gone for good. In his evidence at the original case, Cyril Potts said he sent prints later by post to the Chief Officer, Fred Houlden, but also, tantalisingly, that the photographer in Ballycastle, to whom he took his film for developing and printing, kept copies. Tommy Cecil, the Rathlin diver and historian who first looked into the forgotten *Mendip Range* affair, characteristically went to the lengths of trying to find out who the photographers were in Ballycastle in 1917, on the off-chance descendants could be traced, but to no avail. The photographs, taken a short time apart, showed clear evidence that the *Drake* was in the process of making a big turn to starboard to enter Church Bay. Not under command? In the sense that she was able in attempting to save herself to change course, yes, she was under command, but in the short time that elapsed after she realised what the *Mendip Range* was doing, she had no longer the capability to change it again to avoid another hazard, a collision.

While the photographs have departed from history, Cyril Potts has in a sense returned recently, through the highways and byways of the internet, with census returns, immigration records and so on being digitised and posted online. The hint that he might have been an enterprising young fellow seems confirmed by the happy discovery that he went on to high officer's rank at a young age in some important shipping companies, sailing worldwide, marrying a girl from Doncaster, his home town, in 1928 and settling in Canada. He can last be traced crossing the Atlantic in 1944 with destination given as Fenchurch Street, in an area of the City of London associated with the shipping world. Perhaps the elusive photographs now reside in a descendant's care in Canada!

The *Mendip Range* does not depart from history, as she can be traced later under the name *Grelrosa*. On 28 January 1941, south-west of Rockall, her luck ran out when she was bombed and sunk. Captain Theaker may or may not have been the same man also involved in this next sea war who survived the sinking of the *Castle Harbour* off Trinidad in 1942. He would have been 73, but there cannot have been many Francis Theakers who were Master Mariners; perhaps it was his son.

Captain Radcliffe of the *Drake* became a Rear-Admiral in 1922 and retired as a Vice-Admiral in 1927, after 41 years in the Royal Navy. He spent his latter years in a cottage in the quiet Devon village of Chulmleigh, publishing some verse and short stories, and enjoying tennis and hunting. He passed away on 7 November 1939. He had become a Knight Commander of St Michael and St George, an order of chivalry awarded to those who rendered important service to Commonwealth and foreign countries. It may well be that his command of the first major ship in the new Royal Australian Navy, *Australia*, earned him this honour. And just two months previously, on 10 September 1939, Admiral Sir George King-Hall, a key figure in the establishment of the force, had also died. Perhaps their paths had not crossed since Sydney Harbour on 13 October 1913, when the Admiral, his post as the last Senior Royal Navy Officer in Australia finished, handed over to the new Navy and sailed for England and retirement.

> …I made a general signal from C. - in - C., officers and men of the Home Division to Royal Australian officers and men, wished for their welfare and God Speed. *Australia* replied.

Both men's lives from boyhood had been the Royal Navy. They were sent for training aged only twelve. What a host of colourful incidents all over the world they and Naval boys like them were to encounter!

Above: The wash of the sinking HMS *Drake*.
Below: Partially submerged hull of the *Drake*.
(*Both Tommy Cecil Collection*)

The *St Anthony* salvage vessel working at HMS *Drake*. (*Courtesy of Douglas Cecil*)

Above: The *St Anthony* (left) attending the *Tarv*,
stranded on Rathlin, c1921. (*Patric Stevenson*)
Below: Salvage boat *Mary* anchored in Church Bay.
(*Courtesy of Loughie McQuilkin*)

Above: HMS *Brisk*. (*Imperial War Museum, Q21038*)
Below: The *Mendip Range* on Ballycastle strand. (*Tommy Cecil Collection*)

Above left: Bowl and plate recovered from the *Drake*. (*Courtesy of Babs Connor & Moyle Distract Council / Rathlin Boathouse*)
Above right: HMS *Drake* Challenge Shield. (*Royal Inniskilling Fusiliers Museum*)
Bottom: Cup presented to the 3rd Battalion, Royal Inniskilling Fusiliers by the officers of the *Drake*. (*Royal Inniskilling Fusiliers Museum*)

The *Ella Hewett*. (*David Slinger*)

The *Drake* wreck. (© Crown copyright, photograph taken by Wessex Archaeology)

The *Drake* wreck South Cardinal Buoy. (*Jessica Bates*)

CHAPTER ELEVEN
The Wreck Becomes a Part of Island Life

All the homes on Rathlin are little farms, the kitchen is the centre of the life: hens and chickens, lambs, calves and dogs all walk in and out as they please. Little girls of eight or nine can milk beautifully. The women do a lot of baking – soda bread, barley bread, drop scones – all these are made in quantities daily on the big griddle hanging on a hook over the open fire.

We had tea today in just such a farm near the far west of the island, and I assure you we had a most delightful time. We had brought our tea along with us on our cycles, and I just went to the house to ask for some boiling water. I was received by the woman, Mrs McFall, with the warmest possible welcome and she insisted on our coming into the kitchen to have our tea. 'Yous are welcome a thousand times!' she kept saying again and again, and one could see she really meant it. Poor dear soul!'

Letitia Stevenson who recorded this, her husband Leslie the Church of Ireland Rector and their twelve year-old son Patric, arrived on the island from Sussex in 1920, at about the same time salvage work began on the *Drake*. As quoted at the outset of this book, watching the work of the salvage team was a fascinating early experience for the family on their island sojourn. There was never a chance of refloating her, and it seems as if the Admiralty awarded rights to four different concerns between 1918 and 1930 to retrieve what they could from the upturned hull. It should be remembered that unlike today, a large part of the port side was exposed, and it is said that when lying alongside the wreck in a small boat, it was necessary to use a 30 foot ladder to clamber up on to the flat uppermost part.

The McCausland family of Ballywhite, Portaferry, were prominent local salvors in these decades, and John McCausland, who was born in 1875, arrived to live on Rathlin with his wife Annie and at least one of their five children, William, attended the island school for nine months.

The McCausland headquarters were the old family home on the shores of Strangford Lough – remembered for the garden with an arch of whale jawbones, a souvenir from a west of Ireland job – and they tackled contracts all round Ireland and Scotland. At this time, just after the war, they had even purchased obsolete warships at Chatham and had them towed to Portaferry for breaking up. John was also a director of the Neptune Marine Salvage Company, Glasgow. Their salvage steamer the *Saint Anthony* came to work on the *Drake* and is probably the vessel Letitia Stevenson refers to:

> …a salvage party is at work on her whenever the weather allows. We often hear explosions. On a quay opposite the mail-boat quay are quantities of stuff which have been brought in, huge pieces of steel plates, engines etc., all twisted, torn, broken and rusted – a gruesome sight! A steamer comes from time to time to take it away to sell and we hear that more than a thousand pounds has been realised already. Some time ago, a lot of cordite and gelignite was brought up and lay unprotected near our little church. We often see the diver in his wonderful rig, going off to his job. They have a motor boat the *Mary* to come and go in…

The diver to whom Mrs. Stevenson refers was named Archie Darragh and the *Mary* belonged to him. It is possible he was operating separately from John McCausland, or he may have been employed by him. The *Mary* was a large wooden boat, probably an old fishing boat, and ironically it was blown ashore during a gale and wrecked, too. Another hopeful local salvor was a Robert Gaston of Coleraine. A number of islanders found much-needed extra employment on the salvage work in these needy times, but it could be tense, with the prevailing fear that the magazines might blow up. Very few brass shell cases – for the smaller guns – have been found by sport divers in recent years and it is believed the value of this non-ferrous metal made them a desirable cargo to be shipped out when enough had been raised and they had been rendered harmless. In retrospect, it seems highly irresponsible to allow blasting on the wreck in the 1920s when 50 years later large professional firms were still very concerned when undertaking their own salvage. John McCausland in the 1930s broadcast memories of his salvage adventures on the Northern Ireland wireless: how interesting these would be today!

On one occasion, an islander named Duncan Smyth was accidentally left behind on the wreck when the charge was set to go off. Duncan had the presence of mind to shelter (there were huts on the hull for the team and their equipment) but the boat returning for him had its planks started by the shock and only energetic bailing permitted their return to dry land! On another occasion, a blast hurled a large chunk of metal skywards, coming to earth again two miles away on the road towards Rue Point, near Alley.

Without any documentation, it is impossible to assess what the achievements were of this piecemeal operation. The salvors broke through into the interior of the hull, and it is recorded that the *Saint Anthony* was able to refill her coal bunkers with good Welsh steam coal, so a miners' strike at the time did not delay her work! With the ship lying on her side (by the 1970s she is reported to be upside down) the salvors must have broken through the Krupp armour plating (in itself valuable) then reached the coal bunkers, and then the engine room, where there would be desirable non-ferrous metal – copper pipes, valves, gauges and other components. Stokers' hammers to break coal have been found in the debris, and a huge lump of coal from the *Drake* is pointed out today beside Church Bay. Amazingly, a sport diver found a much more gigantic lump of coal, the size of a table, on which were stamped marks including the crest of the colliery from which it came, as if it was some kind of presentation piece – not for burning – signifying the link with the *Drake* or the Royal Navy in general. Such lumps are indeed known to have been exhibited at trade fairs and suchlike as the pride of the Welsh coal industry.

In a sense the abandoned *Drake* was like the *Marie Celeste*, but without the mystery of where the crew disappeared to and why. Everything bar the ship's official papers was left behind. Steel chests were taken off holding secret books and cipher log signal books and later deposited with the Senior Naval Officer, Buncrana, according to Captain Radcliffe's report. But when sub-aqua diving started becoming a popular hobby, the first enthusiasts who visited the wreck before the Navy largely flattened it in the 1970s reported they could still see uniforms and even men's shaving brushes! Plates and cutlery were easily picked up; the stores compartments full of every kind of spare part were accessible; maker's name plates on pieces of equipment were a nice souvenir; brass portholes were even nicer – and just where did one of the two valuable phosphor bronze propellers go? Very little non-ferrous metal was left by the early 1970s, either removed by the 1920s salvors or later person or persons unknown.

But it is the things that got away which as often happens make the best anecdotes: Tommy Cecil found the compartment with the equipment of the ship's own divers, including an array of helmets, but the Royal Navy blew up this part of the ship before he could raise them. A handsome case containing all the cutlery from the Captain's cabin, stamped with the ship's crest, was lifted by another hopeful diver only to be mistakenly left out for the binmen by the diver's wife! And what became of the ship's bell? Is it the bell now displayed at the present shore depot HMS *Drake* at Portsmouth? No-one seems sure.

Whether or not McCausland and the other salvors had enough impact to reduce the wreck until it ceased showing above the surface is impossible to say, but perhaps more likely it was the settling of the hull into the seabed which meant that, at a date around 1929, the 'great whale' could no longer be seen from shore.

But it was still there, as a British submarine found, to the cost of her Commanding Officer's advancement in the service, in the 1950s. Engaged in exercises in the north-west approaches, and simulating wartime conditions, the submarine's CO decided to confuse his 'enemies' by lying close to the wreck of the *Drake* so that the asdic signal would be misinterpreted as just being a known wreck. It was a cunning plan, too cunning as it turned out, for the submarine ran hard and fast onto the *Drake*, and, humiliatingly, had to be towed off by a destroyer!

But there was no freeing the big deep-water trawler *Ella Hewett*, which snagged the wreck a few years later. It was the night of 5 November 1962, and the *Ella Hewett*, Skipper William Gregson, outward bound from Fleetwood for the Icelandic fishing grounds, was creeping out of Church Bay after the crew had imbibed a last drink, or several, in McCuaig's pub. This was a frequent port of call for the Fleetwood men, although whether the owners always knew is unlikely. Inward bound, the trawlers would exchange fish for cigarettes and their crews were well-known to the islanders. One of the nineteen-strong crew, cook Russell Harvey, suffered leg and chest injuries in a fall when the wreck was struck, and he was taken off by the Portrush lifeboat, along with most of his shipmates. Five men stayed to operate the pumps, but the owners, the Hewett Fishing Co, felt there was too great a risk and they too were taken off. Shortly afterwards, the *Ella Hewett* slipped off the wreck (which was not yet marked with a buoy) and sank alongside it on the landward side. The Liverpool and Glasgow Salvage Association's vessel *Dispenser* was despatched to the scene, but the potential cost of raising the 595 ton trawler was prohibitive.

Attempted disposal, though, of the wreck of the *Ella Hewett* opened the way to a new chapter in the story of the *Drake*, one that has its mysterious side, and which brought the old warship back into the newspapers after nearly 60 years. The trawler wreck was bought by a company named Metal Recoveries (Newhaven) Ltd for £800 and through a new concern named Metrec (Salvage) Ltd, they entered into a joint venture with Shipbreaking (Queenborough) Ltd who were anxious to carry out such operations at Cairnryan in Scotland, only 50 miles from Rathlin. It seems the real prize was the *Drake*. The official owners of the *Drake* were by now the Commissioners of Irish Lights, charged with the responsibility of providing safe lighting and buoyage round the coasts, and they were naturally concerned about the hazard the wreck presented. Metrec were to be allowed to clear the wreck of the warship in order that it could access its property, the trawler. However, concern soon set in about the effect of explosives on the ammunition still aboard the *Drake* and poor weather conditions also hampered the scheme.

In 1968 an old dredger was bought by Metrec at Barrow for conversion to a floating crane for the *Drake*, but by 1970 director Silvio Musmeci was still outlining plans to the press to break up the hull by underwater explosives, after any original munitions had been removed, of course. Matters continued to drag on, and by 1972 it was revealed that most of the non-ferrous metal had disappeared, legally or illegally, over the years (the propeller of the trawler had to be removed to stop amateur divers taking it).

However, unforeseen events on the Northern Ireland mainland were to change the status of the *Drake* dramatically. There seems strong evidence that explosives from the *Drake* were somehow acquired by paramilitaries and used in terrorist explosions in Co Antrim. In the summer of 1974, divers from the Admiralty vessel *Laymoor* apparently removed much of the ammunition still aboard the ship, and in September of that year the Ministry of Defence took over ownership from the Commissioners of Irish Lights – possibly under the Special Powers Act – and unilaterally banned any diving. In September 1976 a huge explosion was detonated in an attempt to flatten the wreck. The last salvage operation is said to have been in 1979 when a Naval diving team blew up more parts of the *Drake*, and the Navy is believed to have interested themselves one way or another in the wreck until the early 1990s. So the saga of the *Drake* certainly did not end when Captain Radcliffe stepped aboard the *Delphinium*! Metrec apparently still owns the salvage rights to the cruiser and the *Ella Hewett*, the badly broken up remains of which are now almost indistinguishable from the warship wreck.

On one of the last Naval missions, island boatman, diver and historian Tommy Cecil was loudly discouraged from helping himself to dead and stunned fish after one explosion. 'These fish are not fit for human consumption!' declared a Naval officer as he hailed him. 'I've a lot of hungry cats!' came the reply!

In 2006, the Northern Ireland Environment Agency engaged the private firm Wessex Archaeology to survey the wreck of the *Drake* to assess whether it was a strong candidate for protection under the Protection of Wrecks Act, 1973. Despite the original torpedo attack and the attempted dispersal of the wreck by the Admiralty, not to mention the ravages of time and the tides, many different features of the old cruiser were identified (a full report is on the company's website.)

The divers found the wreck of the cruiser and the trawler lying on fine sand with frequent scallop and clam shells, heavily covered by kelp and other seaweed and home to pollock, ling, wrasse, edible crabs, starfish and more unfriendly denizens of the deep, conger eels.

The distinctive ram-shaped bow which impaled the *Mendip Range* was recognisable, as was a section of the gallery at the stern where an Admiral aboard – King-Hall in Australia, or Prince Louis of Battenberg – would have taken the air before a pink gin and a splendid dinner. Likewise, the giant rudder, which the crew turned by hand on the last day, was still lying there, and a section of the propeller shaft. Two shells for the secondary armament, the six-inch guns along the ship's side, were spotted, which led Wessex Archaeology to warn sport divers of the dangers still lurking on the *Drake*.

And to the west of the main wreck lay a huge anchor, no doubt the one which splashed into Church Bay at 11.46 am on Tuesday, 2 October 1917, announcing the distressed arrival of the *Drake*, never to leave Rathlin Island again.

EPILOGUE

Loughie McQuilkin talked with enthusiasm about the *Drake*. It was more than 80 years since he had last seen the wreck, in his boyhood, when the 'great whale' which so impressed the Stevenson newcomers still showed above the waves. Now Loughie is one of the last islanders who remembers setting eyes on the hull of HMS *Drake*...

> My father Daniel was what they called a war watcher. Six-hour shifts they had. He was at the East Light, not far from here, on duty with Jamie Glass the day it happened. There were six men stationed there and another six at the upper end of the island. They saw all the action. The lookout was where the old rocket house is in the grounds of the East Light on Altacarry Head. You can see it yet. If there was a message to be sent they'd have to go down to the Post Office in Church Bay who would use Morse Code then...

> ...after a big gale I remember wooden bits off the wreck still floating ashore, and I remember the wooden huts where the salvage workers lived. They're still there you know, on the far side of the Manor House...

The November dusk was dropping down over Rathlin and there was a strong hint of coming winter chill in the wind. But the family home at Coolnagrock, where McQuilkins have lived for more than 50 years, was sheltered and snug.

> ...oh, yes, I remember the *Drake* lying there. I remember them saying that if the waves were starting to break over her, the wind would be sure to go round to the north-west...

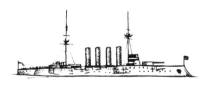

Appendix A: Glossary

Abeam	at right angles to the length and directly opposite the centre of a vessel
Armoured cruiser	obsolete type of cruiser warship, featuring belts of side armour
Barbette	protective circular armour feature around a gun – in the *Drake*'s case, eight sets of guns along the sides of the hull
Belt	layer of heavy metal armour plated onto or within the hulls of warships
Bulkhead	an upright wall within the hull of a ship
C in C	Commander in Chief
Clinker	Incombustible coal residue
CO	Commanding Officer
Cordite	a smokeless explosive used to propel shells without damaging the barrel
Crankpit	base of an engine where the piston rods connected to the cranks revolve to turn the crankshaft powering the propellors
DSC	Distinguished Service Cross
DSO	Distinguished Service Order
HMAS	His Majesty's Australian Ship
HMAY	His Majesty's Armed Yacht
HMS	His Majesty's Ship
HMT	His Majesty's Trawler
HMY	His Majesty's Yacht
Kapitänleutnant	German Naval rank roughly equivalent to Lieutenant in the British Royal Navy
Leutnant	German Naval rank roughly equivalent to Sub-Lieutenant in the British Royal Navy
Lugsail	a type of square sail
LV	Light Vessel
Pinnace	a small vessel used as a tender

Puddler	a wrought iron worker
RFA	Royal Fleet Auxiliary
RMS	Royal Mail Ship
RN	Royal Navy
RNR	Royal Naval Reserve
Salvor	a seaman or engineer engaged in salvage work on a vessel not owned by themselves, and who are not members of the original crew
SMS	Seiner Majestät Schiff (His Majesty's Ship)
SS	Steam Ship
USN	United States Navy
USS	United States Ship
Voicepipe	a device using a sound pipe and two cones for the transmission of speech
Yawing	movement of a vessel's bow from side to side

Appendix B: List of Fatalities
HMS *Drake*

Casualties on the database of the Commonwealth War Graves Commission: HMS Drake

Chatham Naval Memorial, Kent
BROWN, Stoker, JOHN FREDERICK, 4199S, H.M.S. "Drake.", Royal Naval Reserve. Killed in action with submarine in North Channel 2 October 1917. Age 23. Son of Emma Shepherd (formerly Brown) of 10, Railway Row, Shankhouse, Northumberland, and the late John Brown.

BUTTLE, Stoker, WALTER WILLIAM, 1410S, H.M.S. "Drake.", Royal Naval Reserve. Killed in action with submarine in North Channel 2 October 1917.

MURDIE, Stoker, ROBERT, 5252S, H.M.S. "Drake.", Royal Naval Reserve. Killed in action with submarine in North Channel 2 October 1917. Aged 22. Son of John and Elizabeth Murdie, of 88, 9th Row, Ashington, Northumberland.

THOMPSON, Stoker, CHRISTOPHER, 6519S, H.M.S. "Drake.", Royal Naval Reserve. Killed in action with submarine in North Channel 2 October 1917. Age 22. Son of William and Sarah Thompson, of 11, James St., South Shields.

Plymouth Naval Memorial, Devon
BROWN, Stoker 1st Class, CHARLES CONSTANTINE, K/29064, H.M.S. "Drake.", Royal Navy. Killed in action with submarine in North Channel 2 October 1917.

CLARK, Stoker 1st Class, JOHN McLEOD, K/1872, H.M.S. "Drake.", Royal Navy. Killed in action with submarine in North Channel 2 October 1917. Age 27. Brother of Mrs Austin Wilkie, of St. Cyr, Quebec, Canada. Born at Edinburgh.

GARTLAN, Stoker 1st Class, WILLIAM EDWARD, SS/114829, H.M.S. "Drake.", Royal Navy. Killed in action with submarine in

North Channel 2 October 1917. Age 23. Son of Andrew and Ada Gartlan, of 70, Smithdown Lane, Edge Hill, Liverpool.

O'BRIEN, Petty Officer Stoker, ROBERT, 296670, H.M.S. "Drake.", Royal Navy. Killed in action with submarine in North Channel 2 October 1917. Age 33. Son of James and Ellen O'Brien of Strand St., Skerries, Co. Dublin.

STANLEY, Stoker, WILLIAM JOHN, 1699S, H.M.S. "Drake.", Royal Naval Reserve. Killed in action with submarine in North Channel 2 October 1917. Age 31. Son of William John and Alma Eliza Stanley, of Liverpool; husband of Mary Stanley, of 24, Armstrong St., Bootle, Liverpool.

TUMBS, Stoker 1st Class, THOMAS JAMES, K/29448, H.M.S. "Drake.", Royal Navy. Killed in action with submarine in North Channel 2 October 1917. Age 40. Son of the late Charles and Mary Tumbs, of Gorton, Manchester.

WILLEY, Leading Stoker, GEORGE FREDERICK, K/1907, H.M.S. "Drake.", Royal Navy. Killed in action with submarine in North Channel 2 October 1917. AGE 28. Son of Frederick and Lucy Ada Willey, of Pasley Rd., Manor Place, Walworth, London. Awarded Naval General Service Medal (Persian Gulf).

WILLIAMS, Leading Stoker, ROBERT JOHN, 302211, H.M.S. "Drake.", Royal Navy. Killed in action with submarine in North Channel 2 October 1917. Age 34. Son of Lewis and Elizabeth Williams, of 7, Old Post Rd., Holyhead.

Portsmouth Naval Memorial, Hampshire
OLIVER, Stoker 1st Class, JOHN GEORGE, K/28133, H.M.S. "Drake.", Royal Navy. Killed in action with submarine in North Channel 2 October 1917.

PARK, Stoker 1st Class, GODFREY, K/27621, H.M.S. "Drake.", Royal Navy. Killed in action with submarine in North Channel 2 October 1917. Age 30. Son of Alfred and Emma Park, of Conisborough, Rotherham, Yorks.

PATTERSON, Engine Room Artificer 4th Class, JAMES, M/17773, H.M.S. "Drake.", Royal Navy. Killed in action with submarine in North Channel 2 October 1917. AGE 26. Husband of Dorothy Goulden (formerly Patterson), of 3, Oban Rd., Byker, Newcastle-on-Tyne.

SHEARD, Stoker 1st Class, BERTIE, SS/117349, H.M.S. "Drake.", Royal Navy. Killed in action with submarine in North Channel 2 October 1917. Age 20. Son of John James and Annie Bella Sheard, of 29, Green Bank Rd., Altofts, Normanton, Yorks.

STARK, Artificer Engineer, ADOLPHUS EDWARD, H.M.S. "Drake.", Royal Navy. Killed in action with submarine in North Channel 2 October 1917. Age 37. Son of William Stark, of 2, Cyprus Terrace, Adelaide Grove, East Cowes; husband of Marguerita Rosa Stark of Prospect Villa, South Mall, Newport, Isle of Wight.

WHEATLEY, Stoker 1st Class, THOMAS, SS/116149, H.M.S. "Drake.", Royal Navy. Killed in action with submarine in North Channel 2 October 1917. Age 23. Son of Thomas and Rebecca Wheatley, of 93, Skinner St., Stockton-on-Tees.

HMS *Brisk*

Argent, William T, Officers' Steward
Buckingham, John, Acting Petty Officer Stoker
Carthy, Adam, Seaman, RNR
Cooke, George, Officers' Steward, 2nd Class
Cooksey, Albert V, Stoker 1st Class
Dalton, Edwin T, Leading Seaman
Fay, Michael, Stoker 1st Class
Flood, William, Leading Seaman
Godwin, Robert J, Stoker 2nd Class
Gray, Charles H., Leading Telegraphist
Greenham, George, Stoker 2nd Class
Grubb, Albert W, Stoker 1st Class
Hand, George J, Leading Stoker
Hardy, Herbert, Leading Seaman

Hosking, William, Stoker 1st Class
King, Ivor F, Leading Seaman
King, Septimus E, Able Seaman
Knight, Charles S, Leading Seaman
Laxton, Charles E, Able Seaman
Light, George, Able Seaman
MacDonald, Donald B, Signalman, RNVR
Miller, John W, Officers' Steward 3rd Class
Owen, Evan, Stoker 2nd Class
Owens, John, Petty Officer Stoker
Pawley, John T, Acting Petty Officer Stoker
Rogers, Ben, Able Seaman
Rowe, Ernest, Able Seaman
Skingley, Ernest, Stoker 1st Class
Williams, William E, Able Seaman
Withey, Charles H, Able Seaman
Woolley, Albert, Able Seaman

Able Seaman Cyril E Brooke died of his injuries on 31 October 1917

HM Trawler *Earl Lennox*

Borman, Walter W, Engineman, RNR
Coates, Thomas, Deck Hand, RNR
Dalton, Oliver, Engineman, RNR
Ellarby, Charles, 2nd Hand, RNR
Hartley, John F C, Deckhand, RNR
Hubberd, Albert, Deckhand, RNR
Lucas, William T, Trimmer, RNR

Sources and Further Reading

Printed material:

ADM 1/8500/223: Court Martial at Devonport to inquire into the loss of HMS *Drake* [Admiralty file].

Blaney, Jim (1982) 'The Great War and the Ards'. *Journal of the Upper Ards Historical Society*, Vol 6, pp18-22.

Cecil, Tommy (1990) *The Harsh Winds of Rathlin*. Coleraine: Impact.

Holme, Richard (1997) *Cairnryan Military Port 1940-1996*. Wigtown: G C.

Ireland, Bernard (1981) *Cruisers*. London: Hamlyn.

Kemp, Paul (1997) *U-Boats Destroyed*. London: Arms and Armour Press.

King-Hall, Stephen (1951) *My Naval Life*. London: Faber and Faber.

Le Fleming, H M (1962) *Warships of World War One, Vol. 2, Cruisers*. London: Ian Allan.

North, H R (2006) 'The Armoured Cruiser Drake', *Plymouth and South West Maritime Heritage Review*, No 40, pp6-14.

Rogers, Frank (2003) 'The Sinking of the "Drake"'. *The Glynns, Journal of the Glens of Antrim Historical Society*, Vol 31, pp21-35.

Stevenson, Letitia *The Guttering Candle or Life on Rathlin 1920-22*. Edited by P Stevenson about 1970, further editing and typed up by J M Dickson in 1997. Original documents held in Ulster Folk and Transport Museum.

U 79 War Diary: National Archives and Records Service, Washington DC.

Vincent, Henry (c1920) *A Stoker's Log*. London: Jarrolds.

Wintour, John (1981) *Jellicoe*. London: Martin Joseph.

Online material:

HMS *Drake*
en.wikipedia.org/wiki/HMS_Drake_(1901)
en.wikipedia.org/wiki/Drake_class_cruiser
www.worldwar1.co.uk/armoured-cruiser/hms-drake.html
www.northantrim.com/HMSDrake.htm
www.my-secret-northern-ireland.com/hms-drake.html
splash.wessexarch.co.uk/2007/10/19/hms-drake-rathlin-island/
(Extensive information and photographs of the wreck.)

U 79 & U-boats
en.wikipedia.org/wiki/SM_U-79
www.uboat.net/wwi/boats/index.html?boat=79
www.uboat.net/wwi/
en.wikipedia.org/wiki/U-boat_Campaign_(World_War_I)

World War I
www.worldwar1.co.uk/
en.wikipedia.org/wiki/Naval_warfare_of_World_War_I
www.naval-history.net (Extensive database of naval information, including casualty lists and detailed articles.)
1914-1918.invisionzone.com/forums (Home of the Great War Forum, including a wide range of discussions on the war at sea.)

General resources
www.cwgc.org (Commonwealth War Graves Commission, includes a searchable database of WWI casualties.)
www.ancestry.co.uk (Large family history site.)
www.awm.gov.au (Australian War Memorial site.)
www.fleetwood-trawlers.info ('The Bosun's Watch', the online archive for information about shipping from the Lancashire town, including the *Ella Hewett*.)
kinghallconnections.com (Site dedicated to the King-Hall family and their connections with the Royal Navy.)
nhcra-online.org (Website devoted to naval and maritime research and collectibles.)
thepeerage.com (Family history site for the UK's peerage.)

Index

Godrevy Lighthouse, Cornwall, 48
Godwin, Stoker 2nd Class Robert J, 68
Gough-Calthorpe, Admiral, 44
Grace, W G, 2
Gray, Leading Telegraphist Charles H, 68
Gregson, William, 59
Greece, 13, 47
Greek Navy, 7
Greenham, Stoker 2nd Class George, 68
Greer, Rector George S, 20
Grenfell, Field Marshall Lord, 15
Grimsby, Lincolnshire, 34, 44
Grubb, Stoker 1st Class Albert W, 68
'Guttering Candle, The', 1
Gwithian, Cornwall, 48

Halesworth, Suffolk, 11
Halifax, Nova Scotia, 23
Hamburg, Germany, 23
Hampton Roads, Virginia, 24, 36
Hand, Leading Stoker George J, 68
Hardy, Leading Seaman Herbert, 68
Hartley, Deckhand John F C, 69
Harvey, Russell, 59
Harwich, Essex, 17
Hassan, Muhammad Abdullah, 11
Hebrides Islands, 26
Hersing, Otto, 20
Hewett Fishing Co, 59
HH 24 (Convoy), 24-5, 29, 43, 36
Hobart, Tasmania, 10
Hosking, Stoker 1st Class William, 69
Houlden, Chief Officer Fred, 35, 52, 54
House of Lords, 51-2
Hubberd, Deckhand Albert, 69
Hudson River, New York, 12

Iceland, 59
India, 10
Inishtrahull Island, Co Donegal, 26, 40
Inishtrahull Sound, Co Donegal, 28, 40
Irish Sea, 20-1, 38
Islay, 22, 28, 41, 43-4
Isle of Man, 23
Isle of Wight, 36, 39, 49

Japan, 5
Jellicoe, Viscount, 5-7, 14, 33
Jess, Kapitänleutnant Heinrich, 23, 26
Jura, 44
Jutland, Battle of, 5, 7, 11, 17, 19

Kattegat, 19
Kelly's (colliers), 21
Ker, Nini, 7
Ker, Olga, (see King-Hall, Olga)
Kiel, Germany, 18-9, 23
Kiel Canal, 28
King, Leading Seaman Ivor F, 69
King, Able Seaman Septimus E, 69
King-Hall, Admiral George, 7, 9, 10-1, 15, 17-8, 55, 61
King-Hall, Lou, 9
King-Hall, Madge, 9
King-Hall, Olga, 7, 9-10
King-Hall, Stephen, 18-9, 24
Knight Commander of St Michael and St George, 55
Knight, Leading Seaman Charles S, 69
Korea, 5
Krech, Kapitänleutnant, 27
Krupp Arms Works, 4, 58

Lancashire, 20
Land's End, Cornwall, 48
Larne, Co Antrim, 2, 37, 39
Larne Lough, Co Antrim, 27
Las Palmas, Gran Canaria, 6
Laxton, Able Seaman Charles E, 69
Lerwick, Shetland, 26
Lewis, John, 3
Light, Able Seaman George, 69
Littledale, Lieutenant Bernard, 29-30, 40
Liverpool, 24, 38
Liverpool and Glasgow Salvage Association, 60
Livorno, Italy, 7
Lloyd George, Prime Minister David, 23
Loch Ryan, Dumfries and Galloway, 20
'Londonderry Sentinel', 38, 50
Lough Swilly, Co Donegal, 13, 23, 25-7, 29, 36-7, 39
Lowe, Third Officer Thomas, 35, 52
Lucas, Trimmer William T, 69
Luther, Edward, 4

Lydd, Kent, 20

Machrihanish, Kintyre, 22
Malaga, Spain, 13
Malin Head, Co Donegal, 24, 26, 28
Malta, 52
Manor House, Rathlin, 14, 63
Mansell, Rear-Admiral G R, 52
Margy River, Co Antrim, 51
Martin, Captain, 21
MacDonald, Signalman Donald B, 69
McAdam, Miss, 22
McCausland, Annie, 56
McCausland, John, 56-7, 59
McCausland, William, 56
McCauslands (salvors), 56-7
McCuaig's pub, Rathlin, 59
McCurdy, Dympna, 32
McCurdy, John Joe, 33, 36
McDowell, Second Officer John, 35, 52
McFall, Mrs, 56
McQuilkin, Daniel, 63
McQuilkin, Loughie, 63
Mediterranean Sea, 2, 6, 10, 12, 15, 44
Mersey, River, 24, 29
Metal Recoveries (Newhaven) Ltd, 60
Metrec (Salvage) Ltd, 60-1
Miller, Vice-Admiral F S, 27
Miller, Officer's Steward 3rd Class John W, 69
Ministry of Defence, London, 60
Minter, Signal Boatswain Joseph A, 13-4
Montalto, Co Down, 7
Montreal, Canada, 26
Morrison, Patrick, 42
Morse, Commander Harry, 31, 33, 39-40
Mountbatten, Earl, 12
Moville, Co Donegal, 14
Müller, Oberleutnant zur See, 26
Mull of Oa, Islay, 28
Murdie, Stoker Robert, 66
Muscat, Oman, 11
Musmeci, Silvio, 60

Naples, Bay of, Italy, 2, 13
Neptune Marine Salvage Co, 57

Neptune Steam Navigation Co, 52-3
New Caledonia, 9
New Guinea, 16
New York, 2, 12, 24
'New York City Journal', 13
Norfolk, Virginia, 36
Norris, Sir John, 1
North Cape, Norway, 24, 48
North Channel, 27, 45
North Rona, Outer Hebrides, 22
North Sea, 16-7, 19, 28, 46
Northern Ireland, 57, 60
Northern Ireland Environment Agency, 50, 61
Norway, 19, 24

Oak Park, Co Carlow, 11
O'Brien, Petty Officer Stoker Robert, 49, 67
Old Head of Kinsale, Co Cork, 22
Oliver, Stoker 1st Class John George, 67
Olympic Games, 13
Oman, Sultan of, 11
Ottoman Empire, 7
Owen, Stoker 2nd Class Evan, 69
Owens, Stoker Petty Officer John, 50, 69

Pacific Ocean, 16, 24
Pans Rocks, Co Antrim, 51
Park, Stoker 1st Class Godfrey, 67
Parry, Lieutenant G R, 37-8
Patey, Rear-Admiral Sir George, 10
Patterson, Engine Room Artificer 4th Class James, 49, 68
Pawley, Acting Stoker Petty Officer John T, 50, 69
Pearl Harbor, Hawaii, 12
Pembroke Dock, Pembrokeshire, 3-5
Petersson, Gustav, 51
Philadelphia, 7
Plymouth, Devon, 49
Plymouth Naval Memorial, Devon, 66
Pola, Austro-Hungarian Empire, 27
Portaferry, Co Down, 7, 20-1, 56-7
Portavo, Co Down, 7
Portrush, Co Antrim, 14, 59
Portsmouth, Hampshire, 5-6, 10, 13, 20, 49, 59
Portsmouth Naval Memorial, Hampshire, 67
Portugal, 23

Ships and boats